from Writing to Composing

AN INTRODUCTORY COMPOSITION COURSE FOR STUDENTS OF ENGLISH

Beverly Ingram
Carol King

Cambridge University Press
Cambridge
New York   New Rochelle
Melbourne   Sydney

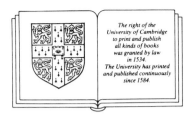

Published by the Press Syndicate of the University of Cambridge
The Pitt Building, Trumpington Street, Cambridge CB2 1RP
32 East 57th Street, New York, NY 10022, USA
10 Stamford Road, Oakleigh, Melbourne 3166, Australia

First published 1988

Printed in the United States of America

Library of Congress Cataloging-in-Publication Data
Ingram, Beverly, 1949–
From writing to composing.
1. English language – Text-books for foreign
speakers.   I. King, Carol, 1947–
II. Title.
PE1128.I477   1987   808′.042   86–33381

ISBN 0 521 33981 2

Contents

iv   Contents

Unit 4   Describing places   66

Unit 5   Describing people   82

Unit 6   Describing people's lives   103

Teachers' notes 119

Appendixes 168

Acknowledgments

We want to express our appreciation to the students, faculty, and administration of The English Language Center at LaGuardia Community College of the City University of New York, the Intensive English Program of the University of Texas at Austin, and the Intensive English Program of the Texas International Education Consortium in the College of Preparatory Studies of the Institut Teknologi MARA in Malaysia. In particular, we would like to thank Linda Austin, Ray Cowart, Gloria Gallingane, Lynn Giudici, Jim Hawkins, Mary Kracklauer, Suma Kurien, Carol Odell, and Kathy Schmitz as well as other teachers too numerous to mention who used early drafts of the materials and made useful suggestions for improving them. We also owe special thanks to Colleen O'Connell and David Moreno, who generously donated their time and energy in creating original artwork for the pilot edition which, though it does not appear here, was an invaluable contribution. And, because their presence is felt on page after page of this book, we want to thank numerous other colleagues in many places for their important contributions to our professional growth and development over the years. We also want to give some personal thank-you's. Carol thanks her mother, Edith King, whose constant love and support have given her the confidence to tackle anything. Beverly thanks her husband, Phillip Sladek, and her parents, Gwen and Truitt Ingram, for their warm, unwavering support through the years and for countless hours of babysitting during this project. Finally, Carol and Bev thank each other for the long friendship and shared experiences that made this book a reality.

The authors and publisher are grateful to the following for permission to reproduce illustrations and photographs: Steve Delmonte (pp. 4, 36, 176 except bottom right, 177 except top left, 178 top left and bottom right); Tom Ickert (pp. 11, 16, 20, 21, 22, 23, 26, 33, 34, 43, 45, 46, 56, 60, 61, 69, 72, 83, 84, 85, 95, 97, 105, 106, 113); Elivia Savadier-Sagov (pp. 78, 176 bottom right, 177 top left, 178 bottom left and top right); J & R Art Services (pp. 67, 71, 94); John F. Kennedy Library (pp. 28, 29); Edward Starr Collection, Department of Special Collections, Mugar Memorial Library, Boston University Libraries (p. 40 top left); Donald S. Pitkin (p. 40 bottom left); The Yomiuri Shimbun, Tokyo (p. 40 top right); Southwest Museum, Los Angeles (p. 40 bottom right); U.S. Department of the Interior, National Park Service, Edison National Historic Site (pp. 53, 90, 105); UPI/Bettmann (p. 103).

Cover design by Dennis M. Arnold
Book design by Peter Ducker

To the Teacher

What is *From Writing to Composing* all about?

From Writing to Composing is a composition textbook for beginning and low-intermediate ESL/EFL students. Through activities ranging from structured "writing" to free "composing," students will become more fluent and confident writers of general-purpose English. Teachers and students can select from a variety of lighthearted and serious topics and activities. Related listening-speaking tasks develop vocabulary, reinforce sound-symbol relationships, and contribute to a lively, motivating classroom atmosphere.

Comprehensive Teachers' Notes, located at the back of this book, contain essential materials that do not appear in the student pages. They also show the teacher how to guide students through simple revision and editing of their compositions. Both student pages and Teachers' Notes offer many ways for students to interact through their writing and about their writing. Two long-range projects, the Class Newspaper Project and the Family History Project, provide a sustained audience, purpose, and outlet for student work.

From Writing to Composing has been field tested in large and small classes worldwide. It is intended for classroom use in intensive, semi-intensive, adult education, university, and secondary school courses.

What does the title *From Writing to Composing* mean?

The title refers to the way we approach teaching composition to lower-level students and the way we have organized the book. Each unit in the book develops one or more topics by moving students from structured "writing" activities to free "composing" activities. Here are the basic differences between these two distinctly different types of activities:

1. A composition is rarely, if ever, finished in one work session, whereas a writing assignment is usually completed on the first try.
2. With composing activities, the teacher should generally ignore, and similarly encourage students to disregard, surface-level problems in grammar and mechanics until the content has been reworked several times and is ready for editing. With writing activities, however, the teacher should expect students to pay close attention to such details and correct the assignments the first and probably only time they are turned in.
3. Composing has a purpose beyond learning the language and an audience other than or in addition to the teacher. A writing assignment, on the other hand, is done only to practice English and only for the teacher's scrutiny.
4. A good composition deserves to be shown off in the class newspaper or on the classroom wall; a writing assignment probably does not.

Because they serve different purposes, "writing" activities and "composing" activities are equally important in a lower-level composition course. Because lower-level students have relatively little language at their disposal, they need a variety of structured writing activities that will give them something to say about a given topic and the language to say it with before confronting a composition assignment on the same topic. Then, after students have put their basic ideas down on paper, they need composing activities that will guide them through the process of rereading, rewriting, revising, and correcting their work until their final compositions communicate their ideas as clearly and accurately as possible.

Why are listening and speaking activities included?

Although the primary purpose of the book is to elicit a great deal of structured and free written work, a strong oral component is essential for lower-level students because they still need basic vocabulary on many common topics. Without oral work, many students would end up doing the structured activities intended to introduce key concepts and vocabulary by merely shuffling around on paper words they had never heard and could not pronounce. When it came time for the students to begin composing, these key words would still not be part of their active vocabulary, and they would be unable to handle the assignment.

Oral activities are also important because of the value lower-level students place on developing conversation skills and because such oral work helps some students overcome their fear of writing. As they talk through an activity, these students often gain confidence to face and eventually conquer their fear of pencil and paper. (At this proficiency level we recommend that students write and compose in pencil, so they can make changes and corrections with ease.)

Why are the Teachers' Notes so extensive? Don't the activities in the student pages speak for themselves?

There is more to a good lower-level composition course than can or should be said to students. The Teachers' Notes explain how to manage the activities in the student pages and also furnish exercises, activities, and ideas that change a book into a course — in short, things that it usually takes a teacher a lot of time to devise. Primarily, then, the Teachers' Notes are meant to save you time. Using them will free you to devote a greater proportion of your preparation time to reading, editing, and reacting to your students' written work.

Even though the Teachers' Notes are not written for students, some of your students may read or attempt to read them. Don't let this worry you. Whatever time and energy they spend looking for "answers" or figuring out what lies ahead will be time and energy well spent. They will benefit more from the experience of wading through more complex English than any incidental exposure to the answers will ever matter.

Should I do the activities in each unit in order, and should I finish one unit completely before beginning another?

The answer to both questions is no. Do *not* take students straight through a unit in order from start to finish. Instead, look over an *entire* unit before planning or teaching even one class session from it. Each unit is composed of several groups of activities, called "sections," which are to be interwoven and overlapped with each other and with activities from the unit that follows. Usually, on any given day in the course, you should have students working on activities from three, four, or five different sections. For example, on a given day, your class might be ready for (1) a follow-up activity on one practice text, (2) a preview activity on another practice text, (3) the first draft of one composition, (4) the editing of another composition, and (5) an Active Vocabulary Practice exercise from the following unit. Whether you could actually undertake this many activities on one day would, however, depend on the length of your class session and the mood and capabilities of your students.

Ideally, you should spend 10 to 15 hours of class time on each unit and finish the book in 12 to 15 weeks. If you have less time, you certainly don't have to cover everything in a unit. You should, however, try to do at least part of every unit. Although the units do become more difficult, some sections, such as the class trip (Unit 4), the survey about the typical student (Unit 5), and the personality profile (Unit 6), should be done at your convenience and not according to their order of appearance in the book. Some activities, particularly the Class Newspaper Project and the Family History Project, once begun should be completed even if that means omitting the rest of the unit.

How can I have my class do a newspaper? I know nothing about journalism.

Neither do we. Journalistic training is not necessary, and producing a professional product is not the point. The goal is to give students a reason to try to write well, a purpose for interacting, and a showcase for their finished work. Although access to a typewriter and photocopy or ditto machine would be handy, you can certainly handle the project quite well without either. Appendix 1 tells you how.

What exactly is the Family History Project?

In the Family History Project each student develops a biographical composition about a family member from the past to preserve for a family member in the future. In each unit, starting with Unit 2, students write, revise, and save paragraphs on given aspects of the past family member's life to integrate in Unit 6 into a composition of lasting value. The project, though challenging, will capture the imagination of your students and give them experience, even at a low level, with the kind of collecting and shaping of material that will be required of them in academic settings.

How should I decide what to do in class and what to assign for homework?

For best results with *From Writing to Composing*, do most composing work in class and as often as possible write along with the students. Spending time *in* class on composing emphasizes its importance, as does your participation as an individual. Both practices send the message that composing is something worth doing. In class, students can't easily ignore or avoid doing composition work, especially when everyone around them, including the teacher, is doing it. When students compose in class, you can observe and intervene in their writing process. When you write, the students can observe your writing process. You should not, however, feel pressure to set an example to be followed. The point to communicate is that even for the teacher, whose proficiency in English is far beyond that of the students, composing requires time, thought, and patience. Even the teacher chews the pencil, stares into space, wads up the paper, and starts again.

For homework, students should routinely produce a half page or so of text in English, principally through structured activities such as those that accompany dictation passages, practice texts, and picture compositions. This controlled type of homework takes relatively little time, so students are more likely to do it. A student who would not go home and write a composition based on a class discussion *will* go home and rewrite a practice text previewed in class. The persistent practice pays off in both expanded vocabulary and improved physical writing fluency. Furthermore, this type of homework is easy for the teacher to mark. By correcting and returning it quickly, you further encourage students to work outside class.

How can I keep the class running smoothly if I have students write in class and they finish at different times?

Since you cannot change the rate at which students write, simply expect that some people will finish ahead of others, and plan what we call "buffer work" to occupy the fast finishers until the class as a whole is ready for the next activity. It is helpful to keep a running list and small file of constructive and rather short activities to serve as buffer work. The Teachers' Notes contain a variety of suggestions. You can have fast finishers complete a homework assignment that you have already begun in class through oral activities. You can also have them do review work by writing previously unassigned variations of structured writing activities. To keep them from perceiving such work as tedious or punitive, however, keep some activities on hand that will seem like a treat or a reward. You might, for example, have students draw classroom display copies of picture cues that you will need in Units 3 and 5. Or, provide a tape player and some taped material in an out-of-the-way corner for students to transcribe, discuss, answer questions about, or react to in some other way. Another way to make buffer work seem appealing is to save copies of especially good papers and have authors recopy them on ditto mats for the whole class. Naturally, as the course progresses, individual conferences about the revision and editing of various works-in-progress are an even better way to fill this time.

How is grammar handled?

From Writing to Composing is not a grammar book. The structured writing activities do not lead students through a progression of grammar points. Students encounter, simultaneously rather than sequentially, these four tenses: the simple present, the present continuous, the simple past, and occasionally the present perfect. The greatest emphasis is, however, on the simple past. Students are expected to gain control of tenses as well as a miscellany of other grammar points through repeated exposure and practice in a variety of writing and composing activities rather than through explicit grammar lessons.

To make the best use of this book, you must be careful in early units not to get sidetracked by the horrendous and frequent grammar mistakes your students will make in their compositions. Although brief explanations of specific grammar points are indeed necessary at times, resist the temptation to take off several days in a row from teaching composition in order to do a thorough grammar review. Instead, move on to new writing and composing activities. The constant flow of new topics will keep students' attention focused on the real goal, communicating meaning, while providing fresh opportunities to practice troublesome grammar points again and again.

My classes have 35 to 40 students. How can I use *From Writing to Composing*?

The activities in this book have been used with classes of all sizes. They worked well. Naturally, how they are managed with a large class is somewhat different than with a small one. (1) A basic recommendation regarding the structured work, which makes up the bulk of the homework, is to check a lot of it orally in class. To keep students on their toes and doing their homework on a daily basis, however, collect and grade everyone's work periodically and without warning. Or, set up a "secret" system for collecting and checking the work of only one-third or one-fourth of the class on any given day. (2) With composing work, always collect and read (but do not mark) everyone's first draft. This is quick to do and will give you an overview of each person's problems and help you select activities useful to everyone. You will of course have to spend considerable time, on a frequent basis, editing and reacting to each person's almost-final and final compositions. (3) With both writing and composing activities, use pair and group work to the maximum to ensure that each person gets a lot of individual interaction time in each class session. (4) To make sure that *you* stay in touch with each person on a regular basis, have students interact with you, and practice their writing skills at the same time, by writing in a dialog journal and turning it in for your reaction on a regular basis. (5) Finally, use the Teachers' Notes that accompany each unit. They are extensive and specific. They will free you from detailed, time-consuming lesson planning and allow you time outside of class to give your students' work the attention it deserves.

Should I have my students buy spirals or looseleaf notebooks for their written work?

We strongly recommend a looseleaf notebook with dividers. Students can file handouts along with their papers in a looseleaf notebook and organize related items together. Dividers are useful because several activities in *From Writing to Composing* require students to retrieve particular papers done in previous units. Also, as the notebook grows in thickness, it serves as a tangible marker of progress that gives a sense of accomplishment, even if it is only thrown away at the end of the course. Furthermore, students' compositions are simply not acceptable in any setting if written on ragged-edged paper torn from a spiral, and if compositions are left in a spiral, it is not easy to exchange or display them. For everyone's efficiency and economy, it is a good idea to coordinate the notebook with the students' other skill-area teachers. Specify enough dividers to make sections for filing students' papers and handouts from all courses, not just those from the composition course.

From Writing to Composing

Unit 1   Getting Started

(see Teachers' Notes on pp. 119–132)

1.1   LETTERS ABOUT PEOPLE: Practice text

Activity A: Interviewing a classmate

1. Write questions to get these facts about a classmate. Work with your class.

2. Work with a partner. Ask your partner the questions. Write the answers on a piece of paper.

3. Introduce your partner to the class. Tell the class about your partner's answers to the questions.

A. Full name: .... ?

B. Birthday: .... ?

C. City, country: .... ?

D. Occupation (in your country/outside class): .... ?
.... ?

E. Length of time here (in this country/city/school): ....
.... ?

F. Reason(s) for studying English: ....
.... ?

G. Plans for the future: ....
.... ?

H. Free-time activities: ....
.... ?

Activity B: Writing a letter about your partner

Write a letter to your family or to a good friend. Write about your partner. Use this framework for your letter.

(date) _____

Dear _____ ,

    I (don't/doesn't/aren't) have much time to write now, but I want to (say/said/saying) hello. I (am/is/are) starting my English class at (school). There (is/are) (number) students in my class. Let me tell you about one of them.

    (full name) is from (city, country). (first name) was born (on/in/at) (year). (she/he) is (a/an) (occupation). (first name) has been here for (number) months. In the future (she/he) plans to _____. (first name) and I will spend (number) hours together each week in this class. Maybe we will become good friends.

    I have to stop now. I hope you are doing well. Say hello to _____ for me. I miss you.

                        (warmly/fondly/love),

                        (sign your name) _____

Activity C: Writing a letter about yourself

1. Work with your class. Talk about this framework for a letter to your teacher. Compare it with the letter in Activity B. What are the similarities? What are the differences?

2. Write a letter about yourself to your teacher. Use this framework. Add the parts that are necessary in a letter.

    My name is _____. I am from _____. (Birthday). (Occupation). (Length of time here). My mailing address is _____.* My phone number is _____.** [OR I don't have a phone. OR I will have a phone (when?) .] (Reasons for studying English). (Plans for the future). (Free-time activities).

*Include the zip code or postal code.

**Include the area code.

1.2 THE BANK ROBBERY: *Picture composition*

Activity A: Matching sentences with pictures

Match each sentence with a picture on page 4, and put the number of the picture (1, 2, 3, or 4) beside the sentence. If a sentence describes more than one picture, use the number of the first appropriate picture.

_____ A. The bank director gives the woman a reward.

_____ B. The woman is making a deposit and cashing a check.

_____ C. She stops him.

_____ D. This man walks to a window.

_____ E. A woman and her grandson are in the bank.

_____ F. The lady hits him with her umbrella.

_____ G. He gets seven balloons from the bank director.

_____ H. He takes two bags of money.

_____ I. A man with a hat is walking in.

_____ J. He starts to run away.

_____ K. A crowd watches.

_____ L. He pulls out a gun.

_____ M. Her handbag and her umbrella are on her arm.

_____ N. She looks happy to get the money.

_____ O. The boy has a balloon on a string.

_____ P. A policeman takes the robber away.

_____ Q. His picture is on the bulletin board.

_____ R. Her grandson also has a smile on his face.

_____ S. He shows a note that asks for money.

Activity B: Putting the sentences in order

Use the sentences in Activity A. Decide which sentence about picture 1 is the first sentence in the story. Put "1A" in the blank beside it. Put "1B" beside the second sentence. Continue with the other sentences about picture 1. Then do the same with the sentences about pictures 2, 3, and 4. Check your answers with the class.

Activity C: Writing the story

Use the sentences and answers in Activities A and B. Write the sentences in the correct order to make a paragraph that tells the story. Use the composition format on page 6.

1.3 REVISING: Format

Activity A: Learning vocabulary about format

This paper has a good format. All readers, including teachers, like papers that have a good format. Identify the parts of this paper. Fill in the blanks with the words beneath the paper.

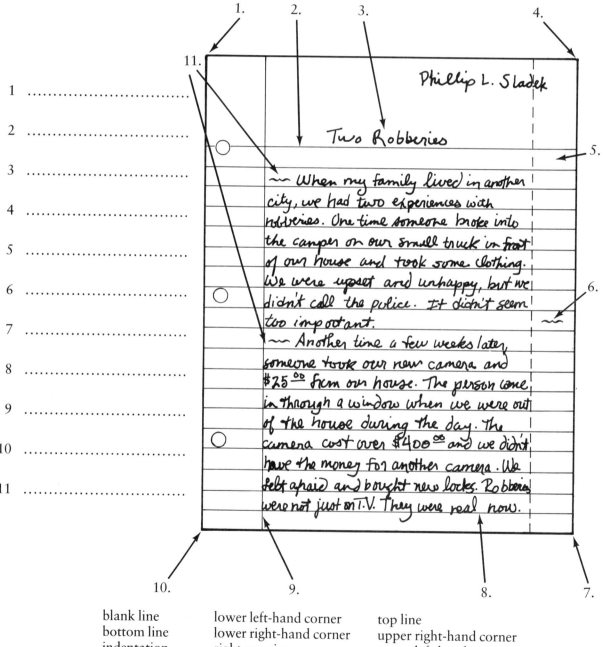

1 ....

2 ....

3 ....

4 ....

5 ....

6 ....

7 ....

8 ....

9 ....

10 ....

11 ....

blank line	lower left-hand corner	top line
bottom line	lower right-hand corner	upper right-hand corner
indentation	right margin	upper left-hand corner
left margin line	title	

Activity B: Finding mistakes in format

This writer made nine mistakes in the format of his paper. Can you find them? Write the mistakes in the blanks. Use the vocabulary in Activity A.

When my family lived in another city We had two experiences with robberies. One time someone broke into the camper on our small truck in front of our house and took some clothing. We were upset and unhappy but we didn't call the police. It didn't seem too important. Another time a few weeks later someone took our new camera and

$25.⁰⁰ from our house.

The person came in through a window when we were out of the house during the day.

The camera cost over $400.⁰⁰, and we didn't have the money for another camera. We felt afraid and bought new locks.

Robberies were not just on T.V. They were real now.

Phillip I. Hladik

1. ....
2. ....
3. ....
4. ....
5. ....

6. ....
7. ....
8. ....
9. ....

1.4   AN UNSUCCESSFUL CRIME: *Practice text*

Activity A: Working with pronouns and verbs

The Bank Robbery

[1]A woman and ▲ grandson ★ in the bank. [2]The woman ★
making a deposit and cashing a check. [3] ▲ handbag and ▲ umbrella ★
on ▲ arm. [4]The boy ★ a balloon on a string. [5]A man with a hat ★
walking in. [6] ▲ picture ★ on the bulletin board. [7]This man ★ to a
window. [8]He ★ out a gun. [9]He ★ a note that asks for money. [10]He
 ★ two bags of money. [11]He ★ to run away. [12]The lady ★ him with
 ▲ umbrella. [13]She ★ him. [14]A policeman ★ the robber away.
[15]A crowd ★ . [16]The bank director ★ the woman a reward. [17]She
 ★ happy to get the money. [18] ▲ grandson also ★ a smile on ▲
face. [19]He ★ seven balloons from the bank director.

▲ = pronoun   ★ = verb

1. Some sentences in the story in the box have one or more blanks with a triangle
   (▲). Each triangle represents a kind of pronoun called a possessive adjective.
   Write the pronouns that are missing in these sentences.

   1. ....
   3. ....
      ....
      ....
   6. ....
   12. ....
   18. ....
      ....

2. Each sentence in the story has a blank with a star (★). Each star represents a missing verb. Write the verb that is missing from each sentence.

1.	8.	15. ....
2.	9.	16. ....
3.	10.	17. ....
4.	11.	18. ....
5.	12.	19. ....
6.	13.	
7.	14.	

3. Practice reading the story aloud. Work with a partner. Cover the pronouns and verbs you wrote. Partner A reads the first sentence, and Partner B uncovers the words to check. Then Partner B reads the second sentence, and Partner A uncovers the words to check. Take turns reading, sentence by sentence, until each partner can read all the sentences correctly.

Activity B: Adding details to the story

Rewrite the story in Activity A to make it more interesting. Add these words in appropriate places. You can use some words more than once.

big	long
black and white	new
famous	old
heavy	teller's
little	young

Activity C: Changing the facts of the story

Rewrite the story in Activity A with these facts: A *man* and his grandson are in the bank. The robber is a *woman*.

Activity D: Writing in the past tense

When you tell a story, you usually tell it in the past tense because it has already happened. Rewrite the story in Activity A in the past tense. Your first sentence will be: "A woman and her grandson were in the bank."

1.5 LETTERS ABOUT THE BANK ROBBERY: *Writing from a point of view*

Activity A: Talking about point of view

It is the *day after* the bank robbery on page 4. Everyone is still thinking about the exciting experience.

1. You are the old lady. You are telling your story in a letter to your best friend.
2. You are the bank teller. You are telling your story in a letter to your sister.
3. You are the bank robber. You are telling your story in a letter to your lawyer.
4. You were in the bank yesterday. You saw the robbery. You are writing a statement for the police, telling what you saw.

Discuss with your class how each of these people felt yesterday and feels now. Then discuss how to begin each letter. When you have decided, your teacher will write your first sentences for each letter on the board.

Activity B: Talking about salutations and closings

1. Here are some common salutations for letters. Which one(s) can be used with each of the letters in Activity A?

   Dear Martha,   Dear Officer Reed:
   Dear Sir: Dear Fred,
   Dear Ms. Jones: Dear Mr. Wilson:

2. Here are some common closings for letters. Which one(s) can be used with each letter in Activity A?

   Sincerely,   Warmly,
   Love,   Yours sincerely,
   Very truly yours,   Fondly,

Activity C: Writing the letter

Work with a partner or small group. Look at the pictures on page 4 again. Then close your book. Finish writing one of the letters in Activity A.

1.6   ACTIVE VOCABULARY PRACTICE: *Basic classroom stretch*

There is an Active Vocabulary Practice section in each unit of the book. These sections will help you learn new vocabulary quickly and follow directions easily. The commands in the box show some of the vocabulary you will practice in this unit. In class, with your books closed, you will act out these and other commands as your teacher gives them.

Stand up.
S-T-R-E-T-C-H.
Touch your toes (nose, hair, chin, right eye, etc.).
Touch both knees (both ankles, both shoulders, etc.).
Touch only your left knee.
Touch your right elbow.
Point to your right elbow.
Touch both ears.
Point to both ears.
Point to the blackboard (bulletin board, map, eraser, wastebasket, ceiling, floor).

Point to the upper (lower) left-hand (right-hand) corner of the blackboard.
Point up (down, to the left, to the teacher, to Joe).
Walk forward (backward). Stop!
Smile. Laugh. Frown.
Make a fist. Shake your fist.
Open your hand.
Point to the palm of your hand.
Hit your forehead with the palm of your hand.
Wave good-bye.
Sit down.

1.7 EXERCISE FOR BUSY PEOPLE: *Practice text*

Activity A: Combining sentences

Combine each group of sentences into one longer sentence. Write the new sentences as a paragraph. Omit all numbers and letters when you write.

Exercise for Busy People

1. a. Today John Jones, a typical worker, has a job inside a building or factory.
    b. The building is tall.
    c. The factory is modern.

2. a. He spends eight hours at work.
    b. He rarely uses his muscles.
    c. The hours are busy.

3. a. He exercises only on weekends at a park.
    b. The weekends are sunny.
    c. The park is nearby.

4. a. A worker such as John needs to get exercise.
    b. The exercise is regular.

5. a. Here are two people who know ways to do this.
    b. The ways are easy.

6. a. A lawyer walks to work every day.
    b. She is important.

7. a. She wears a suit.
    b. She wears jogging shoes.
    c. The suit is expensive.
    d. The shoes are old.

8. a. She carries her shoes in her briefcase.
    b. The shoes are nice.

9. a. An employee of a factory takes breaks.
    b. The factory is big.
    c. The breaks are short.
    d. The breaks are in the morning and afternoon.

10. a. He stretches beside a machine.
    b. He touches his toes beside a machine.
    c. The machine is huge.

11. a. Exercise is important to this man and woman.
    b. It makes them feel better.

Activity B: Making changes in the paragraph

Rewrite the paragraph in Activity A to tell about many people. Your first sentence will begin: "Today typical workers such as John Jones have jobs. . . ."

1.8   REASONS FOR EXERCISING: *Dictation*

Activity A: Dictation

With your book closed, write the paragraph as your teacher dictates. Then open your book. Compare your paragraph with Form A below.

Reasons for Exercising (Form A)

Why does a person exercise? Some people exercise for their cardiovascular health. Other people exercise to burn calories and lose weight. They want to look better. Still other people exercise for fun and relaxation. In fact, most people probably exercise for all three reasons.

Activity B: Talking about the dictation

Part I. Practice with the information in Form A.

1. How many sentences tell about reason one? reason two? reason three?
2. What do some people do to relax and have fun?

Part II. Practice with information related to Form A. If your class cannot answer a question, talk about where to find the answer.

3. Everyone has a cardiovascular system. What are the parts of this system? What does "cardio" mean? What does "vascular" mean?
4. Which food has more calories?
    - a potato or a tomato?
    - a salad or a pizza?
    - an apple or a banana?
    - a piece of chicken or a piece of fish?
    - a cup of milk or a bottle of beer?
5. How many calories does the average adult need each day?

Activity C: Adding information to the dictation

Where does this information fit into Form A? Copy Form A and add the information.

1. ... and build firm muscles
2. They enjoy themselves when they exercise.
3. They want to build strong hearts and circulation.

Activity D: Making a cloze exercise

You must study Form A of the dictation to prepare for the dictation quiz of Form B. You do NOT need to memorize Form A. Form B will have the same vocabulary and the same information, but the sentences will be different.

A good way to study is to make your own *cloze exercise*. In the box below, you see an example of a *cloze*. Notice that the student who made this cloze omitted every 6th word. Cover the answers with a piece of paper. Try to fill in the blanks. Check by uncovering one word at a time.

Now make your own cloze exercise using "Reasons for Exercising (Form A)" on page 13. Omit every 5th word. Practice with your exercise.

Reasons for Exercising

Why does a person exercise? ① _____ people exercise for their cardiovascular ② _____. Other people exercise to burn ③ _____ and lose weight. They want ④ _____ look better. Still other people ⑤ _____ for fun and relaxation. In ⑥ _____, most people probably exercise for ⑦ _____ three reasons.

1. Some
2. health
3. calories
4. to
5. exercise
6. fact
7. all

1.9 EDITING: *Subjects and verbs*

Activity A: Talking about sentences, subjects, and verbs

Do you know what a sentence is? You might say it is a group of words beginning with a capital letter and ending with a period. But a sentence is more than that. Every sentence, long or short, has one or more *subjects* and one or more *verbs*. Study the sample paragraph carefully and discuss it with your class. Sample:

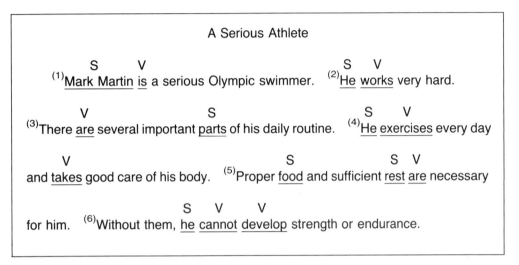

A Serious Athlete

       S   V   S   V
(1)Mark Martin is a serious Olympic swimmer.   (2)He works very hard.

        V   S   S   V
(3)There are several important parts of his daily routine.   (4)He exercises every day

      V   S   S   V
and takes good care of his body.   (5)Proper food and sufficient rest are necessary

                                S   V   V
for him.   (6)Without them, he cannot develop strength or endurance.

Activity B: Identifying subjects and verbs

Underline the subject(s) and verb(s) in each sentence in the next two paragraphs. Then mark each underlined word with "S" for subject or "V" for verb.

Soccer

    (1)Soccer is a good form of exercise.   (2)It is becoming more popular in the United States every year.   (3)Boys and girls play this sport for fun and health.   (4)There are no breaks in the game.   (5)Players run constantly and build endurance.

Sports on TV

    (1)Baseball and football are popular American sports.   (2)There are many professional teams in each sport, and these teams play games on TV.   (3)These days people are watching less baseball because it doesn't have much action.   (4)But football has lots of action and is an exciting game on TV.

Activity C: Finding subject and verb mistakes

Practice making corrections. Write "S" or "V" in the circles to tell what is missing. Then write the missing words beside the circles.

> Football
> ○   ○
> Football ˄a popular sport. But ˄is dangerous. Players often hurt themselves.
> ○   ○
> ˄Need special clothing for safety. Helmets and pads ˄necessary.

Activity D: Finding and adding subjects and verbs

1. Bob wrote this paragraph to give his opinion about sports. What is his opinion? Do you agree with it?

2. Bob's paragraph has some mistakes with subjects and verbs. Underline the subjects and verbs, and mark them with "S" or "V." When a subject or a verb is missing, make a circle and write the missing word in the circle. The first two sentences are marked as examples. (HINT: Six sentences are correct.)

> ### The Truth About Sports
>
> (1)There <u>is</u> too much <u>attention</u> on sports these days. (2)Most <u>sports</u> ⓐⓡⓔ useless
>
> activities, but some <u>people spend</u> a lot of money on them. (3)Sports equipment
>
> and tickets for games becoming more expensive every year. (4)Sports a big
>
> waste of time, too. (5)Athletes usually aren't very smart because don't read and
>
> study enough. (6)Are also very bad for the body. (7)Many people get hurt while
>
> they practicing their favorite sports. (8)They may pull their muscles or break a
>
> leg. (9)Finally, sports lovers usually don't have any friends. (10)Here the
>
> reasons. (11)Normal people don't like them because they sweat and smell
>
> bad. (12)They also very boring because are always talking about one thing –
>
> sports. (13)If they are very good at sports, they often think that they are better
>
> than other people. (14)Of course, aren't! (15)In general, the world would be a
>
> better place without sports.

1.10 AN INTRODUCTION TO THE NEWSPAPER

Activity A: Talking about newspapers

Read the questions, and discuss your answers with the class.

1. Do you read a newspaper in your native language? If so, which newspaper do you read? Why? How often?

2. Do you read a newspaper in English? If so, how often? Which paper? Why?

3. Which parts of the paper do you like to read? Which types of articles and columns do you like?

Activity B: Getting acquainted with newspapers

Work with a partner or small group. Look at a recent newspaper in English. Answer these questions about the newspaper.

1. What is the name of the newspaper? What is its date? How much did it cost?

2. How many articles are on the front page? Copy two headlines from the front page.

3. Can you find an article about a robbery or other crime? If so, where?

4. Where is the weather report?

5. Where is the index? What types of things are listed in the index?

6. Is the newspaper divided into sections? If so, what are the names of the sections?

7. Is there an editorial or an editorial section? If so, where is it? How is an editorial different from other newspaper articles?

8. Is there a crossword puzzle? If so, where?

9. Is there an advice column? If so, where?

10. Can you find a cartoon? If so, where? Are there any comic strips? If so, where?

11. Is there a graph or table? If so, where?

12. Where are the classified ads? What are they?

13. Can you find any other advertisements? If so, where? Why does the newspaper have advertisements?

14. Is there a horoscope? If so, where?

15. Are there any advertisements about exercise clothing or classes? If so, where?

Activity C: Making a classroom display about newspapers

Make a display about newspapers for the wall or bulletin board in your classroom. Cut out an example from the newspaper of the items in this list. Tape the items to a big sheet of paper. Label each item with a colored marker. Work with a small group, and put up your display when you finish.

1. name of paper
2. classified ads
3. crossword puzzle
4. political cartoon
5. advice column
6. advertisement for exercise clothing or classes
7. weather report
8. index
9. comic strip
10. graph or table
11. editorial
12. article about a crime
13. headline about . . . .
14. . . . .
15. . . . .

Activity D: Beginning a class newspaper

In this course, you and your classmates will make a class newspaper. You will write the articles and do the artwork. The first step is choosing a name for your class newspaper.

1. Answer these questions with your class or a small group:
    a. What newspapers in English can you buy?
    b. What newspapers in other languages can you buy?
        Can you translate their names into English?

2. Write three ideas for the name of your class newspaper. Share your ideas with the class. With the class, choose a name for your newspaper.

Activity E: Making a masthead for the class newspaper

1. Bring the front pages of some newspapers to class. Look at the top part of the front page. This part is called the masthead. The masthead always gives the name of the newspaper. Look at the names. Are the names in small letters? What information besides the name of the newspaper is in the masthead?

2. Use a pencil, a ruler, and a piece of standard-sized unlined paper. Follow these directions:
   a. Draw a horizontal line ½ inch from the top of the page.
   b. Draw a horizontal line ½ inch from the bottom of the page.
   c. Draw a vertical line ½ inch from the right edge of the page.
   d. Draw a vertical line ¾ inch from the left edge of the page.
   e. Draw another horizontal line 1½ inches below the top horizontal line.

3. In the area between the two horizontal lines at the top of the page, print or write the name that your class chose for its newspaper. Use large, attractive, dark letters. In the same area, use smaller letters to print or write this information: the course, the year, the name of the school, the city, etc.

1.11 THE STORY OF A CRIME: Composition/newspaper activity

Activity A: Telling a story about a crime

Have you ever seen a crime? Have you heard about one? What about someone you know? What are the names of some crimes?

Work with a partner. Tell your partner the story of a crime. The crime can be big or small. Tell a personal story if possible. If you don't have a personal story, tell about a famous crime or an imaginary one.

Activity B: Writing a story about a crime

Write a story about a crime. Tell all of the story, and give as many details as possible. Work quickly. Follow these rules when you write:

1. Don't worry about mistakes.
2. Don't erase anything. Cross out words or parts you don't want.
3. Don't ask questions of the teacher or other students. They will be writing, too.
4. Don't worry about vocabulary. Leave a blank or use a word from your language if you can't think of the word in English.

1.12   AN INTRODUCTION TO THE COMPOSING PROCESS

Activity A: Talking about how people compose

Look at the two boxes below. Which box shows what happens when you compose? With your class, discuss what is happening in each box.

Box A

Box B

Activity B: Talking about the steps in the composing process

According to writers, composing is much more than just writing. Composing includes thinking, writing, talking, writing, reading, writing, revising, editing, *and* writing again. On page 21 is one diagram of the composing process. Each big box in the diagram shows a step in the process.

1. Which paper (A, B, or C) is the first draft? the second draft? the final paper? Write these names on the papers.

2. Which frame (1, 2, 3, 4, or 5) shows each step?
   - revising   - writing the first draft
   - collecting information   - editing
   - sharing
   Put these names in the blanks beside the numbers.

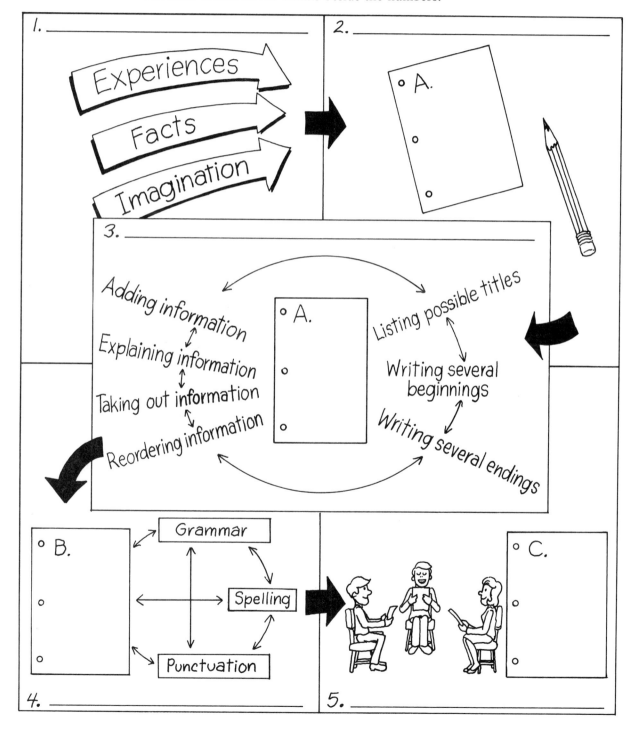

Unit 2 Getting Acquainted

(see Teachers' Notes on pp. 132–137)

2.1 *MEET MY CLASS:* Composition/newspaper activity

Activity A: Learning about averages, minimums, maximums, and ranges

1. Your teacher will read some sentences to you. Listen, and fill in the blanks in the table. Then complete this sentence:

    _____ carries his/her books and papers in a _____ .

Situation: Class members use different kinds of bags for their books and papers.

Tom		John	
	Tote bag		Backpack
W18″ × H10″ × D8″	___ × 11″ × 6″	17″ × 12″ × ___	13″ × ___ × 4″
___ lbs.	2 lbs.	2¼ lbs.	___ lbs.
$15	$12		$12

W = width   H = height   D = depth   ″ = inches   lbs. = pounds

---

2. With a partner make questions and sentences like these:

   - What is the minimum depth? 3½ inches
   - What is the maximum depth? 8 inches
   - The bags range in depth from 3½ inches to 8 inches.

   Talk about *width*, *height*, *weight*, and *price*.

3. Test yourself. Complete these sentences:

   a. The bags range in _____ from 1 to 2¼ pounds.

   b. The bags _____ in width from ___ to 18 inches.

c. The bags range in _____ from 10 inches to 17 inches.

d. The bags _____ in price from _____ to _____.

e. The bags range _____ depth _____ 3½ inches _____ 8 inches.

4. Calculate the following averages with a partner. Follow the example if you need help.

a. average width: _____

b. average height: _____

c. average weight: _____

d. average price: _____

Example: What is the *average* depth?
1. Add the depths:
   8 + 6 + 3.5 + 4 = 21.5
2. How many bags are there? 4
3. Divide 21.5 by 4: 21.5 ÷ 4 = 5.4
   The average depth is 5.4 inches.

Activity B: Working with paragraph organization

1. Match each topic with one of the sentences about an English class.

age   marital status   size of hometown
length of time here   native languages   total number of countries and continents
living situation   occupations   total number of students

.... These students come from cities and towns that range in size from 1,000 to 4 million people.

.... Four of the students are married. Six are single.

.... In their countries they had various occupations. For example, five were students. One was a doctor. Another was a secretary, and another was a mechanic.

.... Ten students, five males and five females, are in the evening English class at West Community College.

.... One student has been here for six years. Another student has been here only two weeks. The average length of time here is four months.

.... They speak the following native languages: Japanese, Spanish, Russian, French, and Swahili.

.... The students range in age from 16 to 55 years. The average age is 32.

.... They come from six countries in Africa, North America, and Europe.

.... Three students live alone. One student lives with a roommate. The other students either live with their spouses and/or with relatives.

⟫→

2. Organize the sentences to make a paragraph.

   a) Which sentence should be first? Why?
   b) Are some of the topics related? That is, do some sentences talk about similar things?
   c) In the left margin write "1" beside the first sentence, "2" beside the second sentence, etc.
   d) Why did you put the sentences in this order? Explain your reasons to the class.

Activity C: Using a chart to collect information

1. Make an information chart on a piece of notebook paper. Follow these instructions.

Instructions for Making Individual Information Charts

A. 1) Fold your paper into thirds (like folding a letter for an envelope).
   2) Fold the paper into thirds AGAIN.
   3) Unfold the paper.
   4) Draw a line along each fold. (How many lines are you going to draw? EIGHT)

B. 1) Fold your paper in half LENGTHWISE.
   2) Fold your paper in half lengthwise AGAIN.
   3) And, AGAIN.
   4) Unfold your paper.
   5) Draw a line along each fold. (How many lines are you going to draw? SEVEN)

C. 1) IMPORTANT! TURN YOUR PAPER SIDEWAYS WITH THE HOLES AT THE TOP. (How many holes are there? How many columns? rows? squares?)
   2) In the square in the upper left-hand corner write the heading "Name." Write "What's your name?" in the square *under* the heading.
   3) In the square to the right of "Name" in the top row, write "Age." In the square *under* "Age" write the question you use to ask a person's age.
   4) Continue across the page writing headings in the top row and questions in the second row. Here are the remaining headings: Length of time here, Living situation, Marital status, Native language, Occupation, Name of hometown and its population, Continent.

D. In the third row answer each question about YOURSELF. For example, under "What's your name?" write YOUR name.

---

2. Work with five or six students to fill in the information charts. The first student asks the second student the questions while the other students listen and write the answers on their charts. Then the second student asks the third student while the others listen and write. Continue in order around your circle.

Activity D: Compiling data

Organize the information from the charts in Activity C. Write the totals and averages for your class (or small group) on the summary sheet.

Summary Sheet

1. Total number of people in the class/group: ....

2. Sex: males: ....   females: ....

3. Age: maximum: ....   minimum: ....   average: ....

4. Occupation: number of students: ....   List four other occupations: ....,
   ...., ..., ...

5. Total number of countries: ....

6. List all of the continents: ....
   ....

7. Native languages: number: .... List them: ....
   ....

8. Largest hometown: ....   population: ....

9. Smallest hometown: ....   population: ....

10. Marital status: married: ....   single: ....   divorced: ....
    separated: ....   widowed: ....

11. Living situation: alone .... with roommate (NOT family): ....
    with family members: ....

12. Length of time here: maximum: ....   minimum: ....
    average: ....

Activity E: Writing a newspaper article about your class

Use the statistics from the class summary sheet in Activity D in a newspaper article. Pay attention to organization. Put related topics together.

2.2 REVISING: "Meet My Class"

Maria wrote the first draft of a newspaper article called "Meet My Class." She read it several times and decided to revise it. She wrote another draft. Read her drafts, and answer the questions.

1. How are the two drafts alike? ....
....

2. How are the two drafts different? ....
....

3. Which draft is better? Why? ....
....

Box A

Meet My Class

Twenty people are in my English class. They come from eight different countries on four continents. They have five native languages. They range in age from 19 to 35. Fifteen of the students are single, and five are married. Three of the students live alone, and two live with roommates. The others live with various members of their families. They are an interesting group of people.

Box B

Meet My Class

Twenty people are in my English class. They range in age from 19 to 35. Fifteen of the students are single, and five are married. They come from eight different countries. Nine of the students live with members of their families. They come from four continents. Three of the students live alone, and two students live with roommates. They are an interesting group of people. They have five native languages.

2.3 *ACTIVE VOCABULARY PRACTICE:* **Mathematics**

Activity A: Simple arithmetic

1. Study the way we write and say these examples.

ADDITION	SUBTRACTION
3 + 2 = 5 or $\begin{array}{r} 3 \\ +2 \\ \hline 5 \end{array}$	8 − 1 = 7 or $\begin{array}{r} 8 \\ -1 \\ \hline 7 \end{array}$
Three <u>plus</u> two equals five.	Eight <u>minus</u> one equals seven.
MULTIPLICATION	DIVISION
4 · 25 = 100 or $\begin{array}{r} 25 \\ \times\ \ 4 \\ \hline 100 \end{array}$ or	12 ÷ 2 = 6 or $2\overline{)12}$ with quotient 6
4 × 25 = 100	Twelve <u>divided by</u> two equals six.
Four <u>times</u> twenty-five equals one hundred.	Two <u>into</u> twelve equals six.

2. Work each problem and write it as a sentence. With the class, read each problem aloud, and tell what type it is (addition, subtraction, multiplication, or division).

a) 10 + 7 = *Ten plus seven equals seventeen (addition).* ....

b) 4 · 5 = ...

c) 3$\overline{)36}$ = ...

d) 11 − 2 = ...

e) 50 ÷ 5 = ...

f) 18,000 × 1 = ...

Activity B: Decimals and fractions

1. Study the way we write and say these examples.

Decimals

a) 3.2 = three point two   *or*   three and two-tenths
b) 3.25 = three point two five   *or*   three and twenty-five hundredths
c) 0.86 = zero point eight six   *or*   eighty-six hundredths

Fractions

a) ½ = one-half   *or*   a half
b) 5⅓ = five and one-third   *or*   five and a third
c) 7¾ = seven and three-fourths   *or*   seven and three quarters

2. Solve each problem. With the class, read the problems and answers aloud.

a) $1.5 + 2.25 =$ ....
d) $½ + ¼ =$ ....
b) $2.5 - 1.3 =$ ....
e) $2 - ⅔ =$ ....
c) $0.5 × 0.3 =$ ....
f) $5 ÷ ½ =$ ....

2.4   THE FAMOUS KENNEDYS: *Dictation*

Activity A: Dictation

Write the paragraph as your teacher dictates. When you are finished, compare what you wrote with Form A in the box.

The Famous Kennedys (Form A)

John and Robert Kennedy were famous brothers. They grew up in a wealthy and powerful New England family. Both entered national politics when they were young. John Kennedy became president of the United States in 1960 at the age of 43. Robert became a candidate for president in 1968. Unfortunately, both of them were assassinated.

Activity B: Talking about the dictation

Part I. Practice with the information in Form A.
1. How are John Kennedy and Robert Kennedy related?
2. In what year was John Kennedy born?
3. How were the lives of John and Robert the same? How were they different?

Part II. Practice with information related to Form A. If your class does not know the answer to one or more of the questions, talk about how you could find out the answers.
4. Do you know which city in the United States is the center of national politics?
5. Do you know where New England is? Which states are in New England?
6. Where, when, and how did John Kennedy die? How about Robert Kennedy?

Activity C: Adding information to the dictation

Copy Form A on a piece of paper, and add this information in logical places.

1. Additional information about John Kennedy:

    — John became a senator from Massachusetts in 1953.
    — John was older than Robert.
    — John died in Dallas, Texas, in 1963.
    — John was the youngest person to be elected president of the U.S.

2. Additional information about Robert Kennedy:

    — Robert became a senator from New York in 1964.
    — Robert died in Los Angeles, California, in 1968.
    — Robert was a candidate for president when he died.

Activity D: Combining information

In the box is a paragraph about Ted Kennedy, the younger brother of John and Robert Kennedy. Combine the information about Ted with the information about John and Robert in Form A. Write one paragraph. Begin your first sentence: "John, Robert, and Ted Kennedy were . . . ."

Ted Kennedy

Ted Kennedy is one of the famous Kennedy brothers. He grew up in New England with his brothers, John and Robert. He also entered national politics when he was young. He became a senator from Massachusetts in 1962.

Activity E: Preparing for the dictation quiz on Form B

Study the structure and spelling in Form A. Make your own cloze exercise using Form A. Omit every 4th word. Cover the answers and practice writing the missing words.

2.5 SIMILAR SIBLINGS: *Practice text*

Activity A: Combining sentences

Combine the following sentences to make a paragraph. Omit the numbers and the letters. Use these patterns:

Tom and Bill
Both Tom and Bill
Both men
Both

Similar Siblings

1. a. Bill is a native Californian.
    b. Tom is a native Californian.

2. a. Tom was born in San Francisco.
    b. Tom was born on October 31, 1958.
    c. Bill was born in San Francisco.
    d. Bill was born on October 31, 1958.

3. a. Tom has curly black hair.
    b. Bill has curly black hair.
    c. Tom has dark brown eyes.
    d. Bill has dark brown eyes.

4. a. Tom is outgoing.
    b. Tom loves to tell jokes to his friends.
    c. Bill is outgoing.
    d. Bill loves to tell jokes to his friends.

5. a. They have good builds.
    b. They are very athletic.

6. a. Bill enjoys all kinds of sports.
    b. Tom enjoys all kinds of sports.

7. a. Bill plays football every weekend.
    b. Tom plays on a soccer team.

8. a. At the university, Bill majored in engineering.
    b. Bill made good grades.
    c. At the university, Tom majored in engineering.
    d. Tom made good grades.

9. a. Bill graduated in 1980 with a B.S. degree.
    b. Tom graduated in 1980 with a B.S. degree.

10. How can two people have so much in common?

11. Of course, they are identical twins.

Activity B: Adding information to the paragraph

Where does the following information fit into "Similar Siblings"? Add these sentences in the logical places.

1. They give lots of parties.
2. Bill was the best student in chemical engineering, and Tom was the best student in electrical engineering.
3. They have five older sisters.
4. They also have dark moustaches and often wear sunglasses.
5. Exercise is an important part of their lives.

2.6 WRITING ABOUT YOUR FAMILY: *Composition*

Activity A: Solving riddles about family relationships

Here are two riddles about family relationships. Can you solve them?

Riddle 1

A man is driving in his car when he sees an automobile accident. He stops to help because he is a doctor. He is very upset when he discovers that the injured person is his son. He takes his son to the hospital as quickly as possible. When the boy is taken into surgery, another doctor enters, looks at the boy, and says, "I can't operate on this boy. He's my son!" How is this possible?

Riddle 2

Two women and their daughters are eating in a restaurant. Only three people are at the table. How is this possible?

Activity B: Preparing questions about families

1. Study the vocabulary in the box. Use your dictionary to look up words that you don't know. If you don't understand something, ask your teacher and classmates.

> parents/relatives   immediate/extended family
> brother/sister-in-law   people
> in-laws   retired
> aunt/uncle/cousin   sibling
> niece/nephew/cousin   spouse
> wife *vs.* housewife
>
> Q. How many people are there in your immediate family, *including you*?
> A. There are five people in my immediate family, *including me*.

⟫→

2. Write questions for these cues. Work with the whole class.

---

1. ...married/single? .... ?

   (...children?) .... ?

2. How many...?

   people .... ?

   brothers and sisters .... ?

   children .... ?

3. Where...live?

   parents .... ?

   brother .... ?

4. What...do?

   mother/father .... ?

   husband/wife .... ?

   brothers and sisters .... ?

5. How often...get together? .... ?

6. Where...get together? .... ?

7. ...most important person...family? Why?

   .... ? Why?

Activity C: Collecting information about families

1. Use the questions you wrote in Activity B to ask about your teacher's family. Try to remember as much as you can, but don't write anything.

2. Bring snapshots (photos) of people in your family to class. Tell a partner about your snapshots and answer questions about them. Find out about your partner's family. Use the questions from Activity B. Try to remember as much as you can, but don't write anything down.

Activity D: Writing to show what you have learned

Test yourself. What did you learn in Activity C? Answer these questions. Check with your teacher and your partner to find out if you remembered correctly.

a. List two things that you learned about your teacher's family.

   1. ....

   2. ....

b. List three things that you learned about your partner's family.

1. ....

2. ....

3. ....

c. How are your family and your partner's family alike?..........................

....

d. How are your family and your partner's family different? ....

....

Activity E: Writing about your family

Without your dictionary, write as much as you can about your family in fifteen minutes. Then spend five minutes reading your work and using your dictionary if you need to.

2.7 *REVISING: "Meet My Family"*

William wrote a composition called "Meet My Family." He wasn't happy with his first draft, so he wrote another one. Read his two drafts, and answer the questions.

1. How are the two drafts alike? ....

....

2. How are the two drafts different? ....

....

3. Which draft is better? Why? ....

....

Box A

> Meet My Family
>
> My parents live in a small town. My younger sister lives at home and goes to high school. My older sister lives in the capital with her husband and studies chemistry at the university. My father works hard as an auto mechanic. My mother teaches elementary school. On Saturdays she works as a secretary. For relaxation my father likes to cook and watch TV. My mother is very busy, but she writes me every week. We sometimes get angry, but we love each other very much. Every person in my family is nice and a little crazy.

⟫→

Box B

Meet My Family

My parents live in a small town. My father works hard as an auto mechanic. For relaxation he likes to cook and watch sports on TV. My mother teaches elementary school. On Saturdays she works as a secretary. She is very busy, but she writes me every week. My younger sister lives at home and goes to high school. My older sister lives in the capital with her husband and studies chemistry at the university. Every person in my family is nice and a little crazy. We sometimes get angry, but we love each other very much.

2.8 *EDITING: Editing symbols*

Activity A: Using editing symbols to make corrections

These students wanted help with some sentences, so their teacher marked the sentences with correction symbols. Help the students by making the corrections. Write each sentence again.

WW	= wrong word	/	= Omit this.
WF	= right word but wrong form	♀	= Add a word.
sp	= spelling error	SV *agr*	= subject-verb agreement
prep	= preposition (for example: in, on, at, under)	⌐	= Change the order of these words.
#	= number; singular ↔ plural		

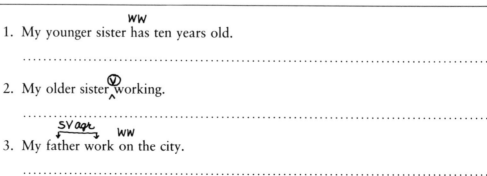

WW
1. My younger sister has ten years old.

....

Ⓥ
2. My older sister working.
          ^

SV *agr*   WW
3. My father work on the city.

....

4. Are four people in my family.

....

SV agr
5. My brother study hard.

....

WF
6. They play with he.

....

SV agr   **Sp**
7. I has many uncles an aunts.

....

SV agr
8. She live at the home.

....

prep   **#**
9. There are my family twenty peoples.

....

WW   **#**
10. My fathers are goods, especially my mother.

....

WF
11. We are live in Toronto now.

....

WF
12. In my family there are three people: my father, my mother, and my.

....

Activity B: Marking mistakes with editing symbols

Each of these sentences has one mistake. Find the mistake, and mark it with the appropriate editing symbol from Activity A.

1. My family have ten people.

2. My oldest brother in the university.

3. My aunt live with my parents.

4. I have two sisters and three brother.

5. My sister studying medicine.

6. My children live now with me.

7. My father has eighty years old.

8. My old sister has three sons.

9. My huband is a student, too.

10. My sisters are work in the city.

2.9 FAMILIES AND FRIENDS AT THE BEACH: Picture composition

Activity A: Matching sentences and pictures

Each sentence tells something about a picture on page 36. In each blank write the number of the correct picture (1, 2, 3, or 4).

_____ A. People are playing volleyball, and someone is water-skiing.

_____ B. The ice chest is in the shade of the beach umbrella.

_____ C. A boy is building a sand castle.

_____ D. A dog is sitting beside a bag of charcoal.

_____ E. A woman in sunglasses is unpacking her car.

_____ F. A woman is taking a nap in her beach chair.

_____ G. People are waving to each other.

_____ H. Two kites are flying in the sky.

_____ I. A man is packing his car.

_____ J. A lifeguard is watching the swimmers.

_____ K. A ship is passing by.

_____ L. Several people are fishing from a boat.

_____ M. A sailboat with a flag is sailing in the distance.

_____ N. People are sunbathing to get a tan.

_____ O. A man with a beard is driving away with a child in the back seat.

_____ P. The garbage cans are full.

_____ Q. A man is cooking hot dogs and hamburgers on a barbecue grill.

_____ R. Someone is upside down in the water.

_____ S. A girl in a dotted swimsuit is holding a pail and a big shell.

_____ T. A beach umbrella is leaning against the side of a car.

Activity B: Planning several stories

The pictures on page 36 give a lot of information, but *you* make them tell a story. In fact, you can make them tell *several* stories. Use the pictures and your *imagination* to fill in the chart. Work with a partner or small group.

	Who?	*Where?*	*When?*	*Why?*
Story One	people who work together		They get together one time every summer.	to meet everyone's family; to get acquainted outside work
Story Two	former neighbors			by accident; to get out of the city
Story Three		near Miami	the last day of the summer season	
Story Four				

Activity C: Evaluating possible titles

Here are nine possible titles for Story One. Which titles do you like the most? Why? Which titles do you like the least? Why? Can you think of other possible titles?

The Beach   A Picnic   A Beach Party
A Day at the Beach   A Nice Day   My Favorite Day Last Summer
A Picnic at the Beach   Fun at the Beach   The Worst Company Picnic

Activity D: Developing characters and plot

Look again at the pictures on page 36. Write three possible answers to each question.

a) Who are the <u>man with a beard</u> and the <u>girl with bows in her hair</u>?

    1. ....
    2. ....
    3. ....

b) If they are father and daughter, why isn't Mom there?

1. ....
2. ....
3. ....

Activity E: Creating your own beach story

1. With your class look again at the chart in Activity B. Write a first sentence for each story that you planned.
2. Work alone. Look at the pictures and the first sentences. Choose ONE story and finish writing it, but DO NOT choose the same story as the classmates near you. Use your imagination and have fun!

2.10 A DAY WITH DAD: Practice text

Activity A: Discussing the paragraph

"A Day with Dad" is one person's story about the beach. Read these questions and look for the answers in the story.

1. Who does Becky probably live with? ....
2. Do Becky and Mike spend every weekend together? ....
3. Where did the Holts and the Browns first meet? ....
4. Which word in the story tells you that there are many people at the beach?

   ....

5. Which two words tell you that Becky and Mike did not plan to meet the Holts

   at the beach? .... , ...

A Day with Dad

Becky Brown's parents are divorced. Becky spends every other weekend with her father, Mike. One Saturday, Becky and Mike decide to go to a beach, and there they get a surprise. Their former neighbors, the Holts, are unpacking the next car. What a coincidence! Everyone waves hello and decides to spend the day together. Mr. Holt finds a spot for them on the crowded beach. During the day some people in the crowd sunbathe to get a tan. Other people swim and play in the water. Still others listen to the radio or pick up shells. Becky covers Mike with sand. The Holts' son, Jimmy, builds a sand castle. Mrs. Holt gets a sunburn. When everyone gets hungry, Mike puts on a chef's hat and cooks hot dogs and hamburgers. Kites and birds fly over the picnic. The families eat and eat. Finally, everyone cleans up, packs the cars, and says good-bye. Becky hugs Mike and falls asleep on the way home.

Activity B: Adding details to the paragraph

Make the story more interesting to read. Rewrite the paragraph, and add the following adjectives. You can use some of the words in more than one place.

bad	delicious	nice	warm
big	favorite	short	wonderful
colorful	hot	tall	

Activity C: Making changes in the paragraph

Becky is an adult now. She remembers a favorite trip to the beach when she was a child. Write her story. Here are the first two sentences: "My parents are divorced. When I was a child, I spent every other weekend with my father, Mike. One Saturday, we . . ."

2.11   BEGINNING THE FAMILY HISTORY PROJECT: *Composition*

Activity A: Introduction

Read this introduction to the family history project with your class. Talk about the questions in it with a partner. Then write your answers to the questions at the end.

Introduction to the Family History Project

Some people are very interested in history; some are not. But most people are very interested in the history of their own families and ask questions about their ancestors: "Where did I come from? Who were my grandparents, my great-grandparents, my great-great-grandparents? What did they do? How did they live?"

Do you know a lot or a little about your ancestors? Which relatives were living when you were born? Which are still living? How many *other* generations of your ancestors do you have any information about? Where did you get this information? Is anyone in your family especially interested in the history of your family? What kinds of family records does your family have? Do you wish you had more information about your ancestors? How can you make sure the future members of your family will know about the history of your family?

In this course, you will write a piece of family history <u>for</u> a future member of your family – maybe your son or daughter, your grandson or granddaughter, your niece or nephew, your cousin. You may write for someone who is very young today, or you may write for someone who has not been born yet.

You will write <u>about</u> one family member, preferably someone who is dead now, but that you know about – perhaps a grandparent, a great-grandparent, an aunt or uncle, or a parent. You must choose a family member that your future reader did not know well.

In this course, you will write about your family member several times and in several different ways. For example, you will write about his or her daily routine, an important place in his or her life, his or her personality and physical appearance, important events in his or her life, and other general biographical information.

Near the end of this course, you will use all these pieces to make one special composition about your family member. You, your classmates, and your teacher will read each other's compositions. You will work together to write clear, interesting pieces of family history. It will be an adventure for you – and for your future reader!

1. Who do you want to write <u>FOR</u>? This person will be your future reader: . . . .

. . . . (name and/or relationship to you) . . . .

2. Who do you want to write <u>ABOUT</u>?

Name: . . . .

Relationship to you: . . . .

Date of death: . . . .   Age at death: . . . .

Activity B: Writing your first thoughts

Write about your family member. Write as much as you can. Do not worry about making mistakes. Write about why you chose this family member for the family history project. Then write everything you know and remember about this person.

Activity C: Working with a fact sheet

This is a fact sheet for collecting information about your family member. Compare your "first thoughts" paper from Activity B with the fact sheet. How many blanks on the fact sheet can you fill with information from your paper? Put a checkmark (√) beside these items and fill in the blanks. Then fill in as many other blanks as possible. Talk with your class about where and how you can get the facts you do not know now.

Fact Sheet About Your Family Member

1. Family member's FULL name: ....

2. Date of birth: .... Place of birth: ....

3. Father's FULL name: ....

4. Father's occupation: ....

5. Mother's FULL name: ....

6. Mother's occupation: ....

7. Number of brothers: ....Number of sisters: ....

   Order of birth (oldest? youngest?): ....

8. Number of years of education: ....

9. Spouse's FULL name: ....

10. Date of marriage: ....Place of marriage: ....

11. Number of sons: .... Number of daughters: ....

12. Occupation: ....

13. Date of death: .... Place of death: ....

    Cause of death: ....

14. Brief description (personality & appearance): ....

    ....

    ....

15. Interests: ....

    ....

16. Community service activities: ....

    ....

17. Famous quotations: ....

    ....

18. Important events in life: ....

    ....

Unit 3   Getting into a Routine

(see Teachers' Notes on pp. 137–143)

3.1   DR. COOK'S DAILY ROUTINE: *Picture composition*

Activity A: Matching

Listen carefully while your teacher tells about each of the 15 pictures in order. Then listen again while your teacher tells about the pictures in scrambled order. This time, in the blanks below the pictures, write the number of each picture when your teacher tells about it.

Situation: Victoria Cook is a young, single woman. She is a doctor and goes to work very early. She gets up about 5 a.m. Every morning she does the same things before work.

1. a) _____   b) _____   c) _____   d) _____   e) _____
2. a) _____   b) _____   c) _____   d) _____   e) _____
3. a) _____   b) _____   c) _____   d) _____   e) _____

Activity B: Writing new vocabulary

Fill in the blanks in these sentences. Each sentence corresponds to the picture in Activity A with the same number.

1. Victoria .... up .... 5 a.m.

2. She.............. out .... bed.

3. She .... to .... bathroom.

4. She .... in.............. ....

5. She .... a.............. .

6. She .... hair.

7. She .... her.............. .

8. She .... out.............. the ....

9. She .... herself .... a towel.

10. She .... hair.

11. She .... her.............. .

12. She .... her.............. .

13. She .... on .... makeup.

14. She .... her.............. .

15. She .... to .... for.............. .

Activity C: Talking about Dr. Cook's routine

Work with a partner. Practice making questions and answers about her routine. Use this framework for your questions:

What does Victoria do just | before / after | she .... ?

Examples: Q: What does Victoria do just *before* she gets out of the tub?
A: She rinses her hair.

Q: What does Victoria do just *after* she gets out of the tub?
A: She dries herself with a towel.

Activity D: Writing sentences with "before" and "after"

1. There are *two* subjects and *two* verbs in each sentence. Mark them as shown. Circle the words "before" and "after."

   a. (After) Victoria gets out of bed, she goes to the bathroom.

   b. Victoria gets up after she wakes up.

   c. She puts on her makeup after she brushes her teeth.

   d. Before she dries her hair, she combs it.

   e. Victoria puts on her clothes before she goes to the kitchen.

2. Two of the sentences above have *commas*. How are these two sentences different from the others? Change the sentences so the commas are not necessary. Write the new sentences here.

   ....

   ....

3. Complete these sentences. Use a comma when necessary.

   Examples: Before Victoria gets out of the tub, *she rinses her hair.* ....

        Victoria rinses her hair ...before she gets out of the tub.

        After Victoria brushes her teeth , *she puts on her makeup.* ...

        Victoria puts on her makeup ...after she brushes her teeth.

   a. After Victoria puts on her clothes ....

   b. .... before she combs her hair.

   c. .... after she gets out of the tub.

   d. Before Victoria goes to the kitchen for breakfast ....

   e. After Victoria wakes up ....

   f. .... before she brushes her teeth.

Activity E: Combining sentences

Put all of the information in Activity B about Victoria's routine into the framework in the box below. Copy your paragraph on a clean sheet of paper.

Victoria Cook's Daily Routine

Every morning Victoria .... up .... 5 a.m. After ....

....

.... shower. .... rinses it before

.... After ....

towel ....

.... makeup.   Then .... before

....

Activity F: Making changes in the paragraph

Victoria's brother lives across town. His name is Victor Cook. He works as a night nurse. He has the same routine before work as Victoria. Last night Victor followed his usual routine. Write about Victor last night. Use the framework in Activity E.

The title: Victor Cook's Routine Last Night
The first sentence: Last night Victor Cook woke up at 9 p.m.

Note: Victoria puts on makeup, but Victor shaves instead.

3.2 JIM STAMP'S DAY: Practice text

Activity A: Learning about Jim Stamp's Day

Fill in the blanks. Work with a partner or small group.

Introduction:

1 Meet Jim Stamp, a handsome man in his forties. For 20 years Jim was a fire
2 fighter (fireman). Then he retired and went to nursing school. Now, Jim and
3 Victor Cook work together. Jim is new at the hospital so he does not have much
4 seniority. He often has to work at night. He describes his working routine.

Jim Stamp's Day

1   I usually wake . . . . at 8:30 or 9 p.m. I . . . . up slowly, take a . . . . ,

2   . . . . , and get dressed. I always put . . . . jeans, a knit sport shirt, and

3   white leather running . . . .   Then I go to the . . . . for

4   something to eat. While I am . . . . , I talk with my wife, Barbara. After my

5   meal, I go into . . . . living room to watch TV with my 13-year-old . . . . , Mike, and

6   my 15-year-old daughter, Angela. Soon, it's time to . . . . for work. Barbara . . . .

7   me in the car. It . . . . us about 15 minutes to get there. As soon as I get to the

8   . . . . , I change into white pants from my locker. . . . . I'm ready for work.

1   My job . . . . at 11 p.m. I check all . . . . my patients and give

2   medications. . . . . I do paperwork. While I . . . . writing, I talk with Victor and

3   Kay, the other night . . . .   Every hour on the hour I . . . . around with a

4   flashlight and . . . . the patients. I also stop at my locker . . . . a quick

5   snack of raisins or crackers. At 1:30 a.m. I take . . . . coffee break, and . . . . it's

6   my turn for a lunch break from 4 to 5 a.m. . . . . I go to the cafeteria, but other

7   times I . . . . a nap. Afterward, I am very . . . . with blood pressures,

8   temperatures, medications, and more .... Finally, at 7:30

9   my job .... I change back into my jeans and ....

the hospital.

1   I take .... bus home. .... I get to the bus stop, I buy a newspaper.   It ....

2   at least 35 minutes to get home, ... I read the paper on the.............. As soon........

3   I get home, I give Barbara a big kiss and .... put on my running clothes.   I run five miles

4   and.............. great.   After I take a shower and have................., I frequently ....

5   things around the house.   Occasionally, I go.................... with Barbara.   After lunch, I

6   start to feel....................... At 2:30 or 3 p.m. I go .... bed.   Mike and Angela

7   .... home from school about that time.   ...., they often forget that..............

8   trying to sleep and make lots .... noise with their radios and records.   Too.............. it

9   is 9 p.m., and I .... start a new day.

1   I don't like.............. work at night, but I'm the .... nurse at the

2   hospital.   I.............. sleep well during the day, so I generally feel ....

3   Most of all, I .... going bowling with my team in the evening.   .... a good

4   bowler, but I .... go bowling when I work at night.   I .... that next year

5   I .... work more during the ....

Activity B: Working with the facts

1. Read each of the statements carefully. In the blank, write "true" or "false." If a statement is false, change it to make it true.

Examples: a. ..*False*....... Jim is ~~20 years old~~. *in his forties.*

b. ..*True*........ Jim prefers to work during the day.

1. .... Jim is a fireman now.

2. .... Barbara is a young nurse who talks to Jim at work.

3. .... Jim spends a lot of time with his children.

4. .... Jim reads a paperback on the bus home.

5. .... Jim rarely goes bowling when he works at night.

6. .... Jim checks his patients every two hours.

〉〉〉→

7. .... Jim's children are teenagers.

8. .... Jim's shift lasts eight and a half hours.

9. .... Jim usually wears jeans at the hospital.

10. .... Jim always eats lunch from 4 to 5 a.m.

2. For each answer, write a question about "Jim Stamp's Day."

   Examples: a. *What does Jim buy every morning* .....? a newspaper

   b. *How old is Jim's daughter* ....? 15 years old

   1. ....? Vic and Kay

   2. ....? at 1:30 a.m.

   3. ....? take a nap.

   4. ....? by bus

   5. ....? five miles

   6. ....? because he
      rarely sleeps well during the day.

   7. ....? Barbara

   8. ....? 35 minutes

   9. ....? at 11 p.m.

   10. ....? raisins or
       crackers

Activity C: Talking about Jim Stamp's day

Work in small groups. Divide the questions among the groups. Take turns asking and answering the questions. Give SHORT answers. After you practice, you will be "experts" and answer your questions in front of the class *without* looking at the book.

1. How old is Jim Stamp? Between ____ and ____ years old.
2. What is Jim's present job? He's a _____.
3. What did he do before he became a nurse? He was a _____.
4. Why does Jim have to work at night? Because _____.
5. When does Jim wake up? At _____.
6. How does he get up? (one word) _____ .
7. What does he wear to work? at work?
8. When does Jim talk to Barbara?
9. When does he watch TV?
10. How does Jim get to work?
11. How long does it take Jim to get to work?
12. What does he do as soon as he gets to the hospital?
13. When does Jim's job start?
14. What does he do while he does paperwork?
15. When does he check the patients?
16. What does he eat for a quick snack?
17. When does he take a coffee break?
18. What does he do during his lunch break?
19. When does he finish work?
20. What does he do before he leaves the hospital?
21. How does Jim get home? By _____.
22. How long does it take Jim to get home?
23. What does he do on the way home?
24. What does he do as soon as he gets home?
25. What does Jim do after his shower and breakfast?
26. When does he go to bed? How long does he sleep?
27. What often happens when Mike and Angela come home?
28. How does Jim generally feel? (one word) _____ .
29. When Jim works at night, what does he miss?
30. What does Jim want to do next year?

Activity D: Writing about Jim Stamp's day

Write for 10 minutes. Write everything you can remember about "Jim Stamp's Day." Write as much as you can.

3.3 *A ROUTINE DAY:* *Composition*

Activity A: Collecting information

Work with a partner. Take turns interviewing each other about your routine day. First, Partner A *closes* the book. Partner B *opens* the book, asks the questions, and takes notes about Partner A's answers. Next, Partner B *closes* the book. Partner A *opens* the book, asks questions, and takes notes on Partner B's answers.

QUESTIONS ABOUT _____ *ROUTINE DAY*
                        (your partner's)

1. When do you wake up? Do you get up immediately?
2. What do you do before you go to school or work?
3. When do you leave your home?
4. How do you get to work or school? What do you do on the way? How long does it take you?
5. When does your work or school start? Are you always on time?
6. What do you do at work or school? When do you take breaks?
7. When does your work or school end? When do you leave?
8. Do you go home right away? If not, what do you do afterward?
9. How do you go home? How long does it take you?
10. When do you get home?
11. What do you do as soon as you get home? Do you always do the same thing?
12. When do you eat? Do you cook? How often do you eat out?
13. What do you do in the evening? Do you always do the same thing?
14. When do you go to bed? Do you go to sleep at once?
15. How long do you sleep?

Activity B: Writing about your partner's routine day

Write a composition with the title: _____ 's Routine Day. Use your notes from Activity A. When you finish, your partner will read your composition and tell you if the *information* is correct and complete.

3.4   *VICTOR COOK'S BREAKFAST: Practice text*

Do you remember Victor Cook? What happens *after* he goes to the kitchen? It is 9:30 p.m. Let's see what Victor is doing now.

Victor Cook's Breakfast

(1)It is 9:30 p.m.   (2)Victor Cook is fixing breakfast before he leaves for work. (3)He is toasting bread in the oven.   (4)He is stirring eggs with one hand.   (5)He is pouring coffee, milk, and juice with the other.   (6)At the same time he is watching the news on TV.   (7)He is also listening to the weather report on the radio.   (8)But he really isn't paying much attention to these things.   (9)He is thinking about his girlfriend, Ellen.   (10)She lives in another city.

Activity A: Writing about Victor's breakfast routine

Victor does the same thing every evening. Write about his daily breakfast routine. Omit the numbers.

The first sentence: Every night at 9:30 p.m. Victor fixes breakfast before he leaves for work.

Activity B: Writing about Victor's breakfast last night

As usual Victor did the same thing last night. Write about his breakfast then. Omit the numbers.

The first sentences: Last night Victor fixed breakfast before he left for work. He toasted bread in the oven.

3.5 *ACTIVE VOCABULARY PRACTICE: Shapes and symbols*

Match the symbols and shapes with their names.

a) _____ ?	1) asterisk
b) _____ ○	2) a capital letter
c) _____ Mr.	3) checkmark
d) _____ □	4) circle
e) _____ %	5) colon
f) _____ good-bye	6) comma
g) _____ B	7) decimal point
h) _____ b	8) diamond
i) _____ ☆	9) dollar sign
j) _____ *	10) equal sign
k) _____ △	11) exclamation mark
l) _____ $	12) heart
m) _____ :	13) hyphen
n) _____ √	14) a lower-case letter
o) _____ 98.6	15) number sign
p) _____ #	16) parentheses
q) _____ =	17) percent sign
r) _____ ▭	18) period
s) _____ ,	19) question mark
t) _____ IV	20) a roman numeral
u) _____ !	21) rectangle
v) _____ ( )	22) square
w) _____ ♡	23) star
x) _____ ◇	24) triangle

3.6 *EDISON'S TYPICAL WORKING DAY:* Dictation

Activity A: Dictation

Write the paragraph as your teacher dictates. When you are finished, compare what you wrote with Form A in the box.

Thomas Alva Edison
1847–1931

Edison's Typical Working Day (Form A)

How did Thomas Edison make over 1,000 inventions? He frequently worked twenty hours out of twenty-four and stopped only for short naps. He ate irregular meals, drank too much coffee, and smoked too many cigars. Despite his unusual daily routine, he lived actively to the age of 84.

Activity B: Talking about the dictation

Part I. Practice with the information in Form A.

1. How much sleep did Edison get in 24 hours? How did he sleep?
2. Did Edison eat regularly? What did Edison like to drink?
3. Why was Edison famous?
4. When was Edison born? When did he die?

Part II. Practice with information related to Form A. If your class does not know the answer to one or more questions, talk about how you could find out the answers.

5. Can you name some of Edison's inventions?
6. Did Edison have a healthy daily routine? Why or why not?
7. The word "despite" shows contrast. Can you write the last sentence in Form A in a different way? Use the word "but."
8. Edison was an inventor. Can you name any other famous inventors?

Activity C: Adding information to the dictation

Where does the following information fit into Form A? Copy Form A on a piece of paper and add these sentences and phrases in the logical places.

1. . . . including the electric light bulb and the phonograph.
2. He said, "Genius is one percent inspiration and ninety-nine percent perspiration."
3. He dressed carelessly and shaved only when he had time.

Activity D: Studying for the dictation quiz on Form B

Study the structure and spelling in Form A. Make your own cloze exercise by omitting every 5th word. Cover the answers, and practice writing the missing words. Then uncover the answers and check your work.

3.7 EDITING: *Fragments*

Activity A: Identifying main clauses and subordinate clauses

A *clause* is a group of words with a subject and a verb. There are two kinds of clauses: main clauses and subordinate clauses. A *main clause* can function as a sentence, but a subordinate clause cannot. A *subordinate clause* is only a *fragment* of a sentence that begins with a word like "before," "after," "if," "when," etc.

Read each clause carefully. If it can function as a sentence, write "main clause" beside it, then capitalize the first word and put a period at the end. If the clause cannot function as a sentence, write "subordinate clause" beside it and circle the introductory word or words. (The first two are examples.)

1. (while) he is eating   *subordinate clause*

2. H̶e doesn't like to work at night ⊙   *main clause*

3. the bus is sometimes late

4. when he gets to the bus stop

5. his coffee break lasts 20 minutes

6. after he takes a shower

7. as soon as he gets home

8. it is time to leave for work

9. their radios make a lot of noise

10. before he goes to bed

11. his job ends at 7:30 a.m.

12. if he is late to work

13. after he checks the patients

14. crackers are his favorite snack

15. because he is new at the hospital

Activity B: Writing sentences with subordinate clauses

A subordinate clause is only a *fragment* of a sentence. First, write a subordinate clause that begins with the given word and has a subject and a verb. Then combine your subordinate clause with a main clause to make a sentence. Write true sentences about Jim Stamp's day. (The first one is an example.)

1. AFTER

   subordinate clause: *after he gets to work*

   sentence: *Jim changes his clothes after he gets to work.*

2. BEFORE

   subordinate clause: ....

   sentence: ....

   ....

3. BECAUSE

   subordinate clause: ....

   sentence: ....

   ....

4. AFTER

   subordinate clause: ....

   sentence: ....

   ....

5. WHEN

   subordinate clause: ....

   sentence: ....

   ....

6. WHILE

   subordinate clause: ....

   sentence: ....

   ....

Activity C: Finding fragment mistakes

This is the editing symbol for sentence fragment mistakes: ( )^F . If a subordinate clause begins with a capital and ends with a period, it is a fragment.

Here is the paragraph that one student wrote about her partner's daily routine. There are 6 fragment mistakes in her paragraph. The first one is marked as an example. Find 5 more fragment mistakes and mark them in the same way.

Glenda's Routine

(After Glenda wakes up.)^F She gets up immediately.   Before she puts on her

clothes, she washes her face.   She eats breakfast.   After she leaves home.

Glenda takes the subway to school.   Before she buys a newspaper.   After her

last class ends at 2 p.m., she goes home.   She usually eats something before

she goes to work.   Because she is hungry.   When she finishes work, Glenda

visits her friends.   Before she goes to bed.   She takes a shower.   She reads a

book.   After she goes to sleep.   Glenda usually sleeps six hours before she

wakes up.

Activity D: Correcting fragment mistakes

Rewrite the paragraph about Glenda's routine in Activity C. Correct all 6 fragments. Add the subordinate clause fragment to the main clause before or after it, or change the subordinate clause into a main clause.

3.8   EDITING: *Editing symbols*

Activity A: Finding mistakes

Lila wrote and revised this paragraph about her partner's routine day. Now she is ready to edit. Read her composition carefully. Then work with a partner. Answer the questions that follow the composition. Discuss your answers with the class.

A Routine Day in Life Joe

1　　He wakes up at 6 o'clock in very morning.　He immediately gets up

2　at once.　He washes your face and putting your clothes.　Then he eats

3　breakfast.　After breakfast.　He usullys leave home 7:30.

4　　He went to school by the subway.　On the train, on your way to school he

5　reading the newspaper.　It takes he fifteen minute get to school, he at

6　school about five hours, his first class begins at nine-fifteen.　and he last class

7　ends at two.　After he goes home.　When he gets home from school eats

8　some thing.　After he go to work.　Then he watch TV listen music and makes

9　homework and some nights he visiting her uncle or friends.　He

10　12 o'clock go to bed.　before he get a shower.　He sometimes

11　in the bed reads book.　Then to sleep.　He usuays sleep 6 hour.

1. Who is Lila's composition about?_____
2. How many times do you find this person's name?_____
3. Can you find a word that is misspelled? On which line(s)?_____
4. Can you find a verb that is not correct? On which line(s)?_____
5. Can you find an example of incorrect punctuation? On which line(s)?_____
6. Can you find a mistake with "after" or "before"? On which line(s)?_____
7. Can you find a sentence that is too long? On which line(s)?_____
8. Can you find a pronoun mistake? On which line(s)?_____
9. Can you find a problem with capitalization? On which line(s)?_____
10. Can you find a sentence fragment? On which line(s)?_____
11. Can you find a sentence with incorrect word order? On which line(s)?_____

Activity B: Learning more editing symbols

Study the editing symbols in the box, and review the symbols in Unit 2 on page 34. Use the editing symbols to correct the mistakes in the sentences. Write the corrected sentences on a clean sheet of paper.

C = Capitalize this word.	*pro agr* = Pronoun agreement mistake.
Ȼ = Don't capitalize.	*poss* = Use possessive form.
P = Punctuation mistake. Add or change the punctuation.	*VT* = Verb tense mistake.
P̸ = Omit punctuation.	*rep* = Repetition.
¶ = Start a new paragraph.	*⌣* = Connect. Make one word.
¶̸ = Don't start a new paragraph.	*( )ᶠ* = Fragment. This is only a part of a sentence.

1. She usuays watches TV at night.

2. Jim works at home, after he eats breakfast.

3. He gets a shower every morning.

4. She goes to School at 8:00 a.m.

5. He puts his clothes before breakfast.

6. She washes your hair every morning.

7. After she does her homework, she watch TV.

8. After work, he goes home and ate a snack.

9. It takes she thirty minutes to walk to school.

10. (After he goes to bed.)ᶠ

11. She washes in the shower her hair.

12. Then listens to music and does her home work.

13. Last night he visiting a friend.

14. He has two class every mornings.

15. Then he goes to the kitchen afterward.

Activity C: Marking mistakes with editing symbols

Each sentence has one mistake. Mark the mistake with the correct editing symbol.

1. He listens the radio every day.

2. He gets out of bed immediately after

   he wake up.

3. She drinks coffee in every morning.

4. Before he leaves home he eats

   breakfast.

5. After he listens to the radio.

6. It takes her two hours to do her
   homeworks.

7. Yesterday he takes the bus to school.

8. He talks to his teacher before goes home.

9. Before bed, she does your homework.

10. He usually walks at class.

Activity D: Correcting mistakes

Look at Lila's composition again. All the mistakes are marked with editing symbols. On a clean sheet of paper, write the final draft of her composition.

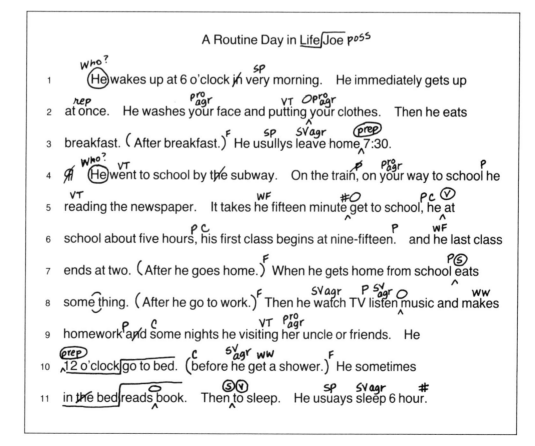

3.9   LETTERS ABOUT A PERFECT ROUTINE: Composition/ newspaper activity

Activity A: Talking about perfect routines

Read the following newspaper article carefully. Talk about it with your class. Tell your classmates some things you do not like about your present routine.

<u>PSYCHOLOGY CORNER</u>

Fast way to a new life

DOCTOR NOE ITALL

Are you tired of your daily routine? Are you bored with your typical days? You <u>can</u> change your life. Here is the important first step.

Use your imagination! Imagine that you <u>now</u> have your perfect routine. You wake up at the perfect time and you eat the perfect breakfast. You put on the perfect clothes. Perhaps you have the perfect job and go to work the perfect way. You have <u>exactly</u> the schedule that <u>you</u> like best. Imagine your perfect days <u>in detail</u> and write to me about this routine. Begin your letter like this: "Dear Dr. Itall, I now have the perfect routine for me. Every morning I..."

When you finish your letter, send it to me. I will read it. Maybe I will show it here in my column. So keep reading "Psychology Corner."

Activity B: Imagining a perfect routine

Spend 10 minutes imagining your perfect routine. Write down your ideas. Do NOT write sentences; write only words and phrases. Work quickly. Write as many ideas as you can. Have fun! Be wild and crazy! Use your sense of humor!

Look at your list of ideas about a perfect routine. Put a checkmark (√) beside some of your favorite ideas. Spend five more minutes thinking about the details of your favorite ideas. Write as many details as you can.

Activity C: Writing a letter about your perfect routine

Write a letter about your perfect routine to Dr. Noe Itall. Use the ideas and details in
your list. Use humor and imagination. Try to make your reader smile and laugh. Start
like this: "Dear Dr. Itall, Now I have a perfect routine. Every morning I. . . ."

3.10 *REVISING: "An Imaginary Day"*

After Kim wrote the first paragraph of her composition, she read it several times.
Then she made some changes and wrote another draft. Read Kim's two drafts, and
answer the questions.

1. How are the drafts alike? ....

2. How are the drafts different? ....

3. Which draft is better? Why? ....

Box A

> ### An Imaginary Day
>
> At 6:15 a.m. soft classical music wakes me up. For five minutes I stretch and
> touch my toes. Then I meditate for 45 minutes in a small, quiet garden beside my
> bedroom. After a hot, lazy shower I put on new jeans and a silk shirt. Next, I have
> whole-wheat toast, fresh orange juice, and hot tea with my husband and son. After
> this delicious breakfast I jump into my pink helicopter and fly over the traffic to
> school. In class I never feel shy when I speak English. After school I push my
> magic button to cook dinner. I exercise and do my homework. In the evening I am
> with my family. We go to bed late because we need only four hours of sleep.

Box B

> ### An Imaginary Day
>
> At 6:15 a.m. I wake up easily. I stretch and meditate for 50 minutes. After
> breakfast with my husband and son, I jump into my pink helicopter and fly to
> school. In ten minutes I am with a wonderful group of classmates. We always do
> our homework, help each other, and enjoy ourselves, too. In class I never feel shy
> when I speak English. After school I fly home and push my magic button. It cleans
> the house and cooks dinner while I swim for an hour. Then I do my homework
> quickly with my computer. In the evening my family and I talk, read, visit friends,
> and play games. We have time for everything because we need only four hours of
> sleep.

3.11 CROSSWORD PUZZLES: Newspaper activity

Activity A: Working a puzzle

Here is a crossword puzzle. Can you work it? Read the questions and write your answers on the grid.

	A	B	C	D	E	F	G	H
1								■
2		■		■	■		■	
3		■			■		■	
4				■				
5	■		■		■			■
6							■	
7		■	■	■	■			
8			■				■	

ACROSS

1A What language are you studying now?
3C What is the opposite of "off"?
4A What is a synonym of "unhappy"?
4E What is another way to write "OK"?
6A What is after first?
7F How much is five minus four?
8A What is the abbreviation of Texas?
8D What does a chicken lay?

DOWN

A1 What is the opposite of "begins"?
A6 The past tense of "sit" is _____.
B4 What is the plural of "is"?
C1 How do you feel when a friend sends you a long, interesting letter?
D5 What is missing?: I always _____ my homework before I watch TV.
F1 How do you feel when your temperature is 102°F?
F6 What animal likes to chase cats?
G4 What is an abbreviation for morning?
H2 What is the fifth month?
H6 How many fingers do you have?

Activity B: Writing cues

Finish this crossword puzzle. Write one question for each word. You will write 10 questions: 4 across and 6 down. Beside each question, you must write the number and letter (1A, D3, F5, etc.) that tells where to write the first letter of the answer.

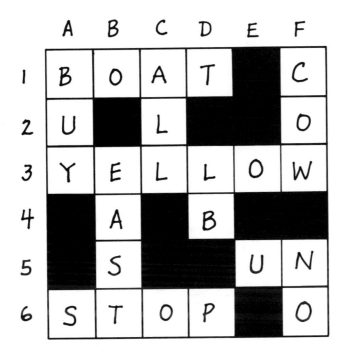

ACROSS

1A ...*What do people use to travel on water?*.................

3A ....

....

....

....

DOWN

A1 ....

....

....

....

....

....

....

Activity C: Making a crossword puzzle

Follow the directions. Make your own crossword puzzle.

Part I
1. Draw a square on lined paper. Each side needs to be approximately 3 inches long.
2. Draw 9 horizontal lines and 9 vertical lines inside the square. Your grid will have 100 boxes (10 across × 10 down).
3. Write the numbers 1 through 10 to the left of your grid. Write the letters A through J above your grid.

Part II
4. Begin to put words in your grid. After you choose a word, write a question for it.
5. IMPORTANT: Each two words touch in only one place.
6. Blacken all the blank boxes.

Part III
7. On a clean sheet of paper, make a clear, neat copy of your puzzle. Write the question cues, but *don't* put the answers on the grid.
8. Exchange puzzles with a classmate. Have fun!
9. Choose the best puzzle(s) in your class, and put it in the class newspaper.

3.12 FAMILY HISTORY PROJECT – ROUTINE DAY: Composition

Activity A: Thinking about the past

History tells about big events, but it also tells about people's ordinary, usual lives. If you want your future reader to know your family member well, you must tell about what he or she did every day.

Think about your family member's life as a teenager. Complete these sentences, and talk about your answers with the class.

In . . . . , when my . . . . was a teenager, life was
        (year)   (family member)
different because . . .

. . . people didn't have inventions such as . . . .

. . . .

. . . people enjoyed doing things like . . . .

. . . .

. . . people worried about . . . .

. . . .

. . . people valued . . . .

. . . .

...people didn't have time-savers such as ....

....

...people had more time for ....

....

...women usually ....

....

...men usually ....

....

...young people usually ....

....

...young people rarely ....

....

Activity B: Making notes about routine activities

Imagine *one* typical day in your family member's *teenage* years. Beside each part of the day, list activities that your family member probably did. Use your knowledge *and* your imagination.

in the morning (6 a.m. – 11 a.m.): ....

....

at midday (11 a.m. – 2 p.m.): ....

....

in the afternoon (2 p.m. – 6 p.m.): ....

....

in the evening (6 p.m. – 8 p.m.): ....

....

at night (8 p.m. – midnight): ....

....

after midnight (midnight – 6 a.m.): ....

....

Activity C: Writing about a teenager's routine day

Write about the typical daily routine of your family member when he or she was a *teenager*. (What verb tense will you use?) Use your ideas from Activities A and B as a starting point. Your future reader will know less about the past than you and will be interested in all the details about this daily routine.

Unit 4 Describing Places

(see Teachers' Notes on pp. 144–151)

4.1 SOUTH AMERICAN NEIGHBORS: Practice text

Activity A: Working with similarities and differences

1. Find Bolivia and Brazil on the map on page 67. With your class answer the questions: How are the two countries alike? How are they different? List all the similarities and differences that you can see on the map or already know.

2. Talk about Bolivia and Brazil. Use the information in your lists with the following patterns. Which patterns show similarities? Which patterns show differences?

> a) Both countries. . . .
> b) Both Bolivia and Brazil. . . .
> c) . . . , but. . . .
> d) . . . ; however, . . .

Activity B: Combining sentences

Combine the following sentences to make a paragraph. Omit the numbers and letters.

South American Neighbors

1. a. Brazil is a country in South America.
   b. Bolivia is a country in South America.

2. a. Brazil is almost as large as the United States.
   b. Bolivia is only one-tenth as big as the United States.

3. a. Brazil has good farmlands, rich mines, and dense forests.
   b. Bolivia has good farmlands, rich mines, and dense forests.

4. a. Brazil has a long coastline, many rivers, and low mountains.
   b. Bolivia has no coastline, few rivers, and many tall mountains.

5. a. The tallest mountain in Bolivia is more than 21,000 feet high.
   b. The highest mountain in Brazil is under 10,000 feet high.

6. a. Brazil lies south of the equator in the tropics.
   b. Bolivia lies south of the equator in the tropics.

7. a. The climate of Brazil is uniformly warm and humid.
   b. The climate of Bolivia varies with the altitude.

8. a. Indians lived in Brazil for many years before any Europeans arrived.
   b. Indians lived in Bolivia for many years before any Europeans arrived.

9. a. The Portuguese settled in Brazil in the fifteenth century.
   b. The Spanish didn't come to Bolivia until the sixteenth century.

10. a. Today Brazil is an independent nation with many natural resources.
    b. Today Bolivia is an independent nation with many natural resources.

11. a. Brazil is working hard to develop its resources.
    b. Bolivia is working hard to develop its resources.

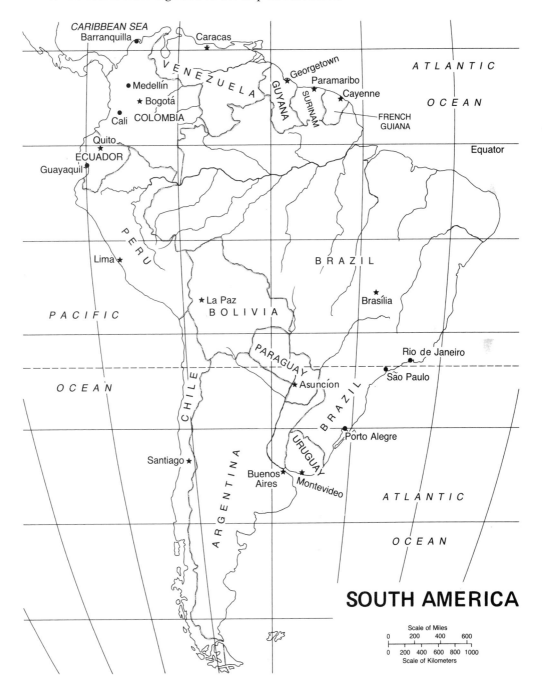

SOUTH AMERICA

4.2   *THE PROUD STATE OF TEXAS:*   *Dictation*

Activity A: Dictation

Write the paragraph as your teacher dictates. When you are finished, compare what you wrote with Form A in the box.

The Proud State of Texas (Form A)

Texas is known around the world for its oil wells, cattle ranches, and cowboys. It is also famous for its size. In fact, Texas is so large that it takes about thirteen hours to drive across it. In 1959, however, Alaska became the forty-ninth and largest state. Proud Texans were upset, so they joked that because Alaska was mainly ice, it could melt. According to them, Texas was still the biggest state.

Activity B: Talking about the dictation

Part I. Practice with information in Form A.

1. What is Texas famous for? (Name four things.)
2. How long does it take to drive across Texas?
3. What word means "unhappy"?
4. When were Texans upset? Why?
5. According to Texans, what was Alaska made of?

Part II. Practice with information related to Form A. If your class does not know the answer to one or more of the questions, talk about how you could find out the answers.

6. How many states are there in the United States? (How many stars are there in the U.S. flag?) Which were the original states? Which one became a state just after Alaska? When did Texas become a state?
7. Approximately how many miles (kilometers) is it across Texas?
8. Texas borders four other states and one country. Can you name them *without* looking at a map? Which language in addition to English is spoken by many Texans?
9. What are some famous Texas cities? What are they famous for? Which city is the capital of Texas?
10. Look at the map of Texas. Can you guess in which part of Texas each of these things can be found?

   – oil wells   – rice fields
   – cattle ranches   – pine forests
   – oranges and grapefruit

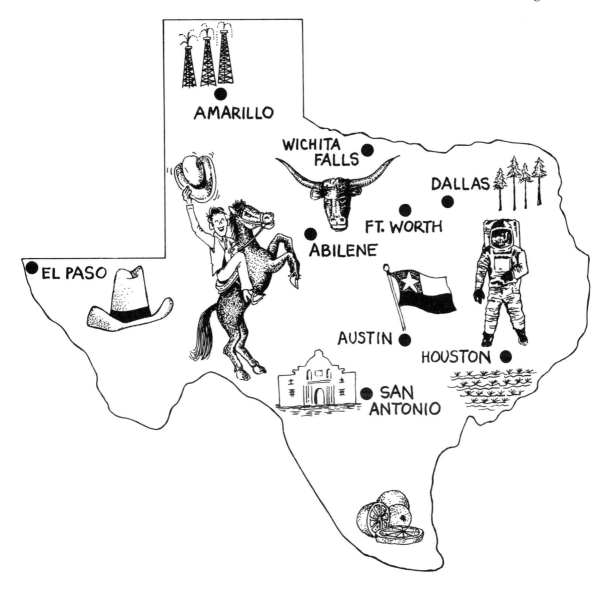

Activity C: Making changes in the dictation

Rewrite the dictation. Substitute each word or phrase in this list for a word or phrase in the dictation with the same or similar meaning.

1. about two days
2. some of them
3. since
4. remained
5. in their opinion
6. everywhere
7. didn't like it at all
8. well known

Activity D: Studying for the dictation quiz on Form B

Study the structure and spelling in Form A. Make your own cloze exercise by omitting every 4th or 5th word. Cover the answers, and practice writing the missing words. Then uncover the answers, and check your work.

4.3 *MY HOMETOWN: Composition/newspaper activity*

Activity A: Finding out about your teacher's hometown

Interview your teacher about his or her hometown. Ask the *underlined* questions in the box. Listen carefully to the answers.

Some Questions About Your Hometown

1. What is the name of your hometown?
2. In what part of your country is it?
3. Describe the geography of your hometown. Is it flat / hilly / in the mountains / in a valley / in a desert / on the coast? Is the land rocky / sandy / good for farming / good for ranching? Are there trees? Is there a river or a lake nearby? Is there a good harbor for ships?
4. Describe the weather and climate. How many seasons are there? What is the weather and temperature in each season? Does it rain or snow? How much? What is the best time of year?
5. How many people live in your hometown?
6. What are the common occupations? What do most people do for a living? What are the principal industries and products?
7. What do people do for entertainment?
8. Is your hometown a good place to visit? Why or why not? What should a tourist see there? What is your hometown famous for?
9. What do you like about your hometown? What do you dislike about it? Does it have any problems? If so, what are they?
10. On the whole, is it a good place to live?

Activity B: Interviewing a classmate

1. Interview a partner about his or her hometown. Use the questions in the box. (*Partner A closes* the book. *Partner B looks* at the book and asks the questions. Partner A answers.) Then exchange roles with your partner.

2. In five minutes, write as much as you can about your partner's hometown.

3. Exchange papers with your partner. Check the information about your hometown. Tell your partner about any mistakes in content that you find.

Activity C: Writing about your hometown

Write a paragraph about your hometown. Use the questions in the box as a guide.

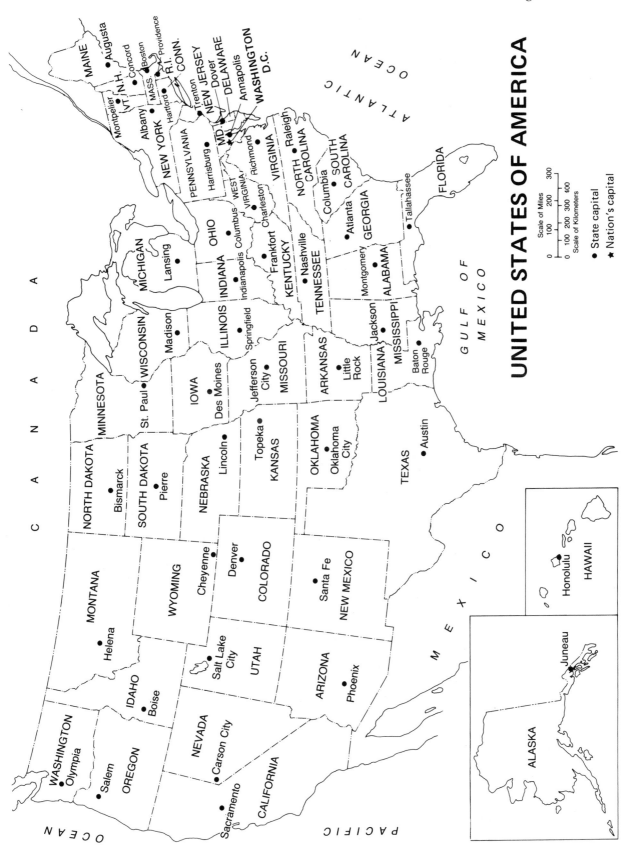

UNITED STATES OF AMERICA

4.4 REVISING: "My City"

Stanley wrote the first draft of a composition called "My City." He read it several times. He wasn't sure about it, so he wrote another draft. Read his drafts, and answer the questions.

1. How are the drafts alike? ....

....

2. How are the drafts different? ....

....

3. Which draft is better? Why? ....

....

Box A

My City

    My city's name is Athens. It has good geography and good weather. For example, the climate is nice. It is a big city. Many people live in Athens. They work there in many things, such as different occupations and different industries. The people enjoy different entertainment. They like to do different things for fun and relaxation. I like my city because it has many famous things to see. It also has many museums and good places to visit. In general, all tourists like my city very much. For instance, they like the well-known places to visit. I love my city because it is a good place to live, work, and play.

Box B

My City

    My city's name is Athens. In my city there are four seasons. The best time of year is spring. In Athens live three million people. Most of them work in offices, factories, and stores. My city is a good place to visit because the weather is very good, the people are very friendly, and there are many exciting places for tourists. Athens has many museums. It also has famous things to see. Two examples are the Acropolis and the Parthenon. My city is also well known because many famous people, such as Socrates, Aristotle, and Pericles, lived there.

4.5 EDITING: *Punctuation*

Activity A: Changing meaning with punctuation

Punctuation is important. It can change meaning. Work with your class. Add commas, periods, and/or capitals to each sentence.

1. The travel agent called Joan Gordon Ellen Carter and me.
    a) How many people did the travel agent call? ....
    b) Rewrite the sentence to show that the agent called five people. ....
       ....
       ....
    c) Rewrite the sentence to show that the agent called three people. ....
       ....
       ....

2. Roger was born in France on September 7, 1970 he went to Canada to work with his brother.
    a) What happened on September 7, 1970? ....
    b) Rewrite the sentence to show when Roger was born. ....
       ....
       ....
    c) Rewrite the sentence to show when Roger went to Canada. ....
       ....
       ....

Activity B: Solving a punctuation riddle

Joe had a ticket for a trip from Chicago to Toronto. Add punctuation to each paragraph about Joe to make it true.

From Place to Place (I)

Joe walked into the plane before the flight attendant closed the door he walked out when the plane landed where was Joe he was in Toronto

From Place to Place (II)

Joe walked into the plane before the flight attendant closed the door he walked out when the plane landed where was Joe he was still in Chicago

4.6 *EDITING:*   Run-ons

Activity A: Learning about a ''run-on''

Here is a new editing symbol: (   )^R . It means the writer did not use capitals and periods to mark the beginning and end of all the sentences. Rewrite the run-ons as shown in the example:

Example: (The geography in my hometown is interesting, the land to the east is flat and good for farming, to the west it is hilly and rocky.)^R

The geography in my hometown is interesting.
The land to the east is flat and good for
farming. To the west it is hilly and
rocky.

1. (The common occupations in my hometown are university employee and government worker, many people also make electronic equipment, others sell insurance or work in stores.)^R

....

....

....

....

....

2. (For entertainment people like to spend time outdoors, swimming, boating, and fishing are popular, many people ride bicycles for fun, people also have picnics at the lakes.)^R

....

....

....

....

....

Activity B: Finding and correcting problems

1. Cover the symbols. Read each line of the paragraph in the box carefully. Look for the problems. Put a check (√) near each problem.

   Examples:

poss
cover→ s-v agr

   My city name is Ottawa.
   The people has many occupation.

2. Uncover the symbols. Compare them with your checks. Did you find all the problems on each line?
3. Rewrite the paragraph. Make the necessary changes. Use the symbols and checks for help.

COVER↓

WF	My city is a excellent place to
sp, Ⓢ∧	live. I thing is wonderful. It has
ww, Ⓢ∧, art∧	very people. Is important city
Ⓢ∧, sp	because is the center of goberment.
Ⓢ∧, ww	Is also great because of yours
⌐, R(	museums very famous. The weather
	in my city is nice, in the
Ⓢ∧	summer is warm and sometimes
)R	rains, in the winter it is cool.
⌐, adv.∧	I very like my city.

4.7   HOMETOWN WEATHER REPORT: *Newspaper activity*

Activity A: Talking about temperature scales

Work with a small group, and then with the whole class. Answer these questions.

$$104°F = 40°C$$

1. Look at the temperatures in the box. What do the small circles mean? What does "F" mean? What does "C" mean?
2. At what temperature Celsius (centigrade) does water freeze? At what point does it boil?
3. What is the boiling point of water on the Fahrenheit scale? What is the freezing point of water on this scale?
4. On the Celsius scale, how many degrees are there between freezing and boiling? On the Fahrenheit scale?
5. Complete the proportion (ratio) between the Celsius and the Fahrenheit scales:

$$\frac{C}{F} = \frac{100 \text{ degrees between freezing and boiling}}{180 \text{ degrees between freezing and boiling}} = \frac{100}{180} = \frac{10}{18} = \frac{?}{9}$$

Activity B: Practicing temperature conversions

When you change Celsius to Fahrenheit or vice versa, you must remember that the Fahrenheit scale starts at 32°, not 0°. Therefore, you must add or subtract 32°, depending on which change you are making. Study the information in the boxes. Then practice making conversions.

To Change Fahrenheit to Celsius

$$\frac{5(F - 32)}{9} = C \qquad \text{OR} \qquad \text{Subtract 32 from degrees of Fahrenheit and multiply by 5. Then divide by 9.}$$

To Change Celsius to Fahrenheit

$$\frac{9C}{5} + 32 = F \qquad \text{OR} \qquad \text{Multiply Celsius degrees by 9, divide by 5, and add 32.}$$

1. Change 100°C to Fahrenheit.
2. Change 32°F to Celsius.
3. Normal body temperature is 98.6°F. What is it in Celsius?
4. Imagine that the weather forecaster on the radio predicted a low tonight of 10°C. What is the predicted low in Fahrenheit?

Activity C: Collecting information

Complete the statements in the box.

In my opinion, the best weather in _____,
                                                                     (my city)

_____, occurs in _____ .
      (my country)   (month)

In this month:

a) The skies are clear / partly sunny / partly cloudy / overcast.

b) The daytime high temperature is _____°C (_____°F).

c) The low temperature at night is _____°C (_____°F).

d) The humidity is _____%.

Activity D: Making a weather report

Follow these steps to make a weather report for your newspaper.

1. Draw a square or rectangle in the space available in your newspaper for the weather report.

2. Label it "Today's Weather." (If you have more space available on another page of your newspaper, use the title "Tomorrow's Weather" for a second weather report.)

3. Print in the information about skies, daytime high, low tonight, and humidity.

4. Draw something attractive, such as a sun, clouds, an umbrella, etc.

5. At the bottom print "P.S. If you like today's (tomorrow's) weather, go to _____(city)_____ , _____(country)_____ , in _____(month)_____ ."

6. Just below the square, print "Reporter: _____(your name)_____ ."

4.8 SURVEY OF FAVORITE CITIES: *Newspaper activity*

Activity A: Organizing the survey

You and your classmates are going to interview fluent English speakers (native speakers, if possible) about their favorite cities or towns. You will read all of the answers in the class newspaper.

Work with your class. Answer these questions:

1. Which English speaker will each person interview?
2. Where and when will you talk to this person? Will you use the telephone? Will you need to make an appointment?
3. Help the teacher make a list of *who* everyone will interview, *where*, and *when*.

Activity B: Practicing for your interview

With your classmates and teacher, plan and perform possible conversations with the English speaker. If possible, also record and transcribe one or more of these conversations. Include these points in the role plays:

— Practice introducing yourself.
— Practice telling your purpose.
— Practice making an appointment for later if necessary.
— Practice getting the information: What is your favorite city or town? Why?
— Practice what to say when you don't understand or need help.
— Practice thanking the person.
— Practice ending the conversation.

Activity C: Doing the interview and writing it up

1. Interview the English speaker. Write down his or her full name. Check the spelling! Write down his or her answers as exactly as possible.
2. Write a short report on your interview. Include the full name of the English speaker, the time and the place of the interview, and, of course, the English speaker's answers.

4.9   A TRIP TO TOKYO: Practice text

Activity A: Making changes in paragraphs

Tina and her husband Ted are now in Tokyo. Rewrite the paragraph to tell about both of them. Begin your first sentence: "Tina and Ted . . . "

A Trip to Tokyo

Tina is spending her vacation in Tokyo. She is wearing her sunglasses and carrying her camera. She is doing everything that tourists like to do. She is visiting museums, shopping in expensive stores, and walking through beautiful gardens. She is also going to famous restaurants. She is staying in the apartment of a friend who is taking her vacation out of the city. Tina is enjoying herself very much, but she is also spending all her money!

Activity B: Writing about her annual vacation

Tina goes to Tokyo every year. Write about her annual vacation. Start with: "Every year Tina . . . "

Activity C: Writing about their annual vacation

Ted goes on vacation with Tina every year. Write about their annual vacation. Begin with: "Every year Ted and Tina . . . "

4.10   ACTIVE VOCABULARY PRACTICE: *Following directions**

Follow the directions in the box. Work by yourself.

Part One

First, take a sheet of paper out of your notebook. Print your name with capital letters in the upper right-hand corner, last name first. Then write the date in the upper left-hand corner, and put the title, "The Seasons of the Year," in the middle of the top line. Finally, number from one to four along the left-hand margin.

Part Two

First, write the names of the seasons of the year beside the numbers. Put "winter" beside number 1, "spring" beside number 2, etc. After that, circle "summer." Underline "fall." Draw a line through "winter." Put an X on number 3. Then draw a rectangle around "spring" and draw a triangle beside "fall." Also, draw a square to the right of "winter," and put a checkmark in the square. Finally, put a check to the left of number 4.

Part Three

First, sign your name in the lower right-hand corner on the bottom line. Next, fold your paper into sixths. Finally, sign your name again on the outside, and write the date above it.

Part Four

Give your paper to the teacher.

---

*Referred to as Exercise 5 in the Teachers' Notes.

4.11   CLASS TRIP: Composition/newspaper activity

Activity A: Choosing a place of interest

Take a trip with your teacher(s) and classmates. Go to a museum, zoo, park, amusement park, sports event, skating rink, restaurant, interesting neighborhood, monument, tourist attraction, etc. Have a meal together if possible. Speak English during the trip!

1. Work with a partner or small group. Brainstorm about places of interest that would be good for a class trip. Make a list of your ideas:

a. ....   f. ....

b. ....   g. ....

c. ....   h. ....

d. ....   i. ....

e. ....   j. ....

2. Work with your whole class. Share your best ideas from the list. Choose the place for your class trip.

Activity B: Planning the trip

Discuss these points with your class.

– date of the trip
– time of departure and return
– cost (of transportation? of admission ticket? of meal or snack?)
– clothing
– place to eat
– type of transportation
– place to meet
– things to take (camera? umbrella? sports equipment? food? swimsuit?)
– people to invite (other teachers? family members? roommates?)

Activity C: Writing about the trip

After your trip, write a short report that tells where you went and what you did.

4.12   *FAMILY HISTORY PROJECT – IMPORTANT PLACE:* Composition

Activity A: Making a list of places

1. Read the family history papers you wrote in Units 2 and 3. Make a list of all the places you mentioned.

2. Add to your list other important places in the life of your family member. Think about where this person was born, grew up, went to school, married, raised a family, worked, spent older years, and died.

Activity B: Writing about an important place

1. Choose one place from your list that was very important in the life of your family member. Fill in the blanks.

   a) name of place: ....

   b) # of years spent there: ....

   c) dates there: ....

   d) age while there: ....

2. Write a description of this important place in your family member's life. Be sure to include the information in the blanks.

Unit 5   Describing People

(see Teachers' Notes on pp. 152–159)

5.1   LETTER TO A HOST FAMILY: Composition

Activity A: Talking about the advertisement

Read the magazine advertisement. Discuss these questions with your class, and list your ideas on the board:

– What would a host family want to know about a future guest?
– What questions might they ask?

Activity B: Writing a letter about yourself

Answer the ad. Write a letter describing yourself for a host family.

5.2 DESCRIBING OTHER PEOPLE: *Dialog*

Activity A: Learning a dialog

After you learn the dialog orally with your teacher and class, fill in the blanks with the words you learned. Then cover the words and use the picture cues to practice the dialog with a partner.

Situation: Mark and Annie, two friends, are chatting at the laundromat while they are doing their laundry.

1. Annie: Have you ever _____ my sister, Sue?

   Mark: No, but I'd _____ to. _____ she _____ _____ you?

   Annie: Not at _____. She doesn't _____ anyone in our family.

2. Mark: Well, _____ does she _____ _____ ?

   Annie: Let's _____. She _____ long _____ blond hair, _____ brown eyes, and a good _____ .

3. Mark: Wow! She sounds _____ ! _____ she _____?

   Annie: She's smart _____ friendly and _____ a great _____ of _____ .

4. Mark: What a fantastic _____ ! What _____ your sister _____?

   Annie: Hmm ... Lots of things ... country _____ , old _____ , and _____ , but she sprained _____ _____ last week.

5. Mark: Gee, _____ too bad. How _____ _____ now?

   Annie: Oh, she's _____ better. _____ you _____ to meet her?

6. Mark: Yeah. Do you think _____ go out with me?

   Annie: I _____ it! She's happily _____ and _____ three _____ .

Activity B: Studying vocabulary

Answer these questions about the dialog.

1. Which word means "intelligent"? ....
2. Which word means "outgoing"? ....
3. Which phrase means "funny"? ....
4. Which word means "children"? ....
5. Which word is the antonym of "straight"? ....
6. Which is the full form of these contractions?

    I'd ....
    What's ....
    She'd ....
    She's ....
    That's ....

Activity C: Matching questions with their meaning

Find five questions about Sue in the dialog. Copy them beside the appropriate labels.

Interests ....
Personality ....
Physical appearance ....
Temporary condition ....
Resemblance ....

Activity D: Matching questions and answers

Annie asks some questions about Mark's brother. Put the letter of Mark's answer in the blank beside Annie's question.

...... Who does he look like?

...... What does he look like?

...... What is he like?

...... What does he like?

...... What does he dislike?

...... How is he these days?

a) He looks exhausted. He's very busy at work and needs a vacation.

b) Baseball, Italian food, video games, and classical music.

c) He has dark hair and eyes. He's not tall, but he is muscular and has broad shoulders. He's really good-looking!

d) He's a little shy, but he's fun to be with. He's very understanding and has lots of common sense.

e) We don't look much alike. In general, he resembles my father's side of the family, but he has my mother's eyes.

f) He hates being early, and he gets bored with watching TV.

5.3 SURVEY ABOUT THE TYPICAL STUDENT: Newspaper article and thank-you letter

Activity A: Practicing adverbs of frequency

Match the arrows with the corresponding adverbs of frequency. For example: I <u>never</u> eat breakfast. = I eat breakfast <u>0% of the time</u>.

almost always	never	seldom
almost never	occasionally	sometimes
always	often	usually
frequently	rarely	

0%	10%	20%	30%	40%	50%	60%	70%	80%	90%	100%
↑	↑	↑		↑		↑		↑		↑ ↑
①	②	③		④		⑤		⑥		⑦ ⑧

1 *never* ....

2 ....

3 a) ....

 b) ....

4 a) ....

 b) ....

5 a) ....

 b) ....

6 ....

7 ....

8 ....

Activity B: Collecting data

1. Look at the "Typical Student Survey Form" on pages 86–7. You will use this form to interview another student and collect data for a newspaper article. For each of the 25 cues, write a complete question. Work with a partner.

》》→

2. Answer the questions on the survey form with information about *yourself.* Write your answers in the column "You." Be sure to record answers of "zero," too!

3. Interview another student. Write the student's answers in the column "Your Partner."

4. Work with your class. Compile statistics from *all* of the answers on *all* of the survey forms.
   — For questions such as "weight" and "# of brothers and sisters," calculate the *average* of the answers.
   — For questions such as "hair color" and "transportation," find the total for each possible answer and use the *largest.*

TYPICAL STUDENT SURVEY FORM

	You	Your Partner
1. Name: _____ (first) (last) 1. Name: _____ (first) (last)		
2. eye color (B = blue, Bk = black, Bn = brown, Gr = green, G = gray)		
3. hair color (Bk, Bn, G, R, Bd)		
4. hair type (S = straight, C = curly, W = wavy)		
5. weight (in pounds) (You don't have to tell the truth!)		
6. height (in feet and inches)		
7. personality (Q = quiet, O = outgoing or talkative)		
8. favorite kind of music (R&R, P, C, T, C&W, J)*		
9. # of brothers and sisters		
10. neighborhood/area of town		

11. type of transportation to class (C, B, Bi, T, W)**		
12. length of time to get to class (in minutes)		
13. # of letters per month to family members in other places		
14. # of phone calls per month to family members in other places		
15. # of movies per month (in a theater)		
16. # of cups of coffee/sodas daily		
17. # of cigarettes/hamburgers/pieces of gum daily		
18. # of hours of TV daily		

*R&R = rock'n roll, P = popular, C = classical, T = traditional, C&W = country and western, J = jazz
**C = car, B = bus, Bi = bike, T = train, W = walk

Answer questions 19–25 by pointing to a place on the line. Then write the percentage in the column at the right.

0%   10%   20%   30%   40%   50%   60%   70%   80%   90%   100%

19. How often .... get up before 6 a.m.?		
20. .... arrive on time for class?		
21. .... eat out?		
22. .... eat alone?		
23. .... to bed before midnight?		
24. .... the radio while you go to sleep?		
25. .... ONLY English all day?		

Activity C: Writing the article

Put the statistics that you and your classmates collected into this framework. Work with a partner. Read the article aloud, and fill in the blanks orally as you read. Write the completed article on your own paper.

★ = verb   # = a number   ▲ = adverb of frequency

What is the typical (level? program?) student like? We did a survey of __#__ students to find out. Here is a description of the typical student according to our survey.

The average (level? program?) student __★__ (eyes) and (hair). S/he __★__ (height) and __★__ (weight). S/he __★__ a _____ personality and __★__ _____ music. S/he __★__ from a family with __#__ children and __★__ (in/near) (neighborhood/area of town). S/he __★__ (transportation) to (name of school). The trip __★__ him/her (length of time). Every month s/he __★__ __#__ letters and __★__ __#__ phone calls to family members in other places, and __★__ to __#__ movies. Daily, s/he __★__ __#__ cups of coffee, __★__ __#__ cigarettes, and __★__ __#__ hours of TV. S/he __▲__ __★__ before 6 a.m. and/but __▲__ __★__ on time to class. S/he __▲__ eats out and/but __▲__ eats alone. S/he __▲__ __★__ to bed before/after midnight and/but __▲__ __★__ to the radio while s/he __★__ to sleep. Finally, s/he has some happy/sad/surprising news for his/her English teacher. S/he __▲__ __★__ only English all day.

Activity D: Making changes in paragraphs

Last year the statistics about the typical student were somewhat different. Write another paragraph, and use last year's statistics in the box. Your first sentence: "Last year, the average .... student had gray eyes and straight, red hair."

Last Year's Statistics: The Typical Student

eyes: gray	letters: 3.6
hair: red	calls: 5.3
straight	neighborhood: near the university
weight: 119.6 lbs.	personality: outgoing
height: 5'4¼"	transportation: walk
brothers and sisters: 3.9	length of time to class: 17 minutes

coffee: 1.6 cups	restaurant: 80% of the time
cigarettes: 6.5	alone: 65% of the time
TV: 2.3 hours	before midnight: 96% of the time
movies: 1.3	radio: 0% of the time
before 6 a.m.: 10% of the time	only English: 45% of the time
on time: 95% of the time	music: classical

Activity E: Writing a thank-you letter

Use this framework to write a thank-you letter to the person that you interviewed in the typical student survey. Talk with your class about words to put into the framework. Write your letter on unlined paper. Fold the letter and address it like an envelope. Deliver the letter to your survey partner.

> (date)
>
> Dear _____ ,
>   My classmates and I really appreciate _____. We used the information to _____. We are sending you _____ and hope you enjoy _____. Thank _____ for _____.
>
>   Sincerely,
>
>   (your signature)

> your full name
> class
> room
> school
>
>   [stamp]
>
>   your partner's first + last name
>   class
>   room
>   school

5.4   *THOMAS ALVA EDISON: Dictation*

Activity A: Dictation

Write the paragraph as your teacher dictates. Then open your book and compare what you wrote with Form A.

Thomas Alva Edison (Form A)

Thomas Alva Edison went to school for only three months, but he loved books, had an excellent memory, and was intensely curious about everything. Almost deaf, this attractive man with pale blue eyes had remarkable energy and determination. He was a practical organizer who constantly asked questions from his childhood until his death.

Activity B: Identifying subjects and verbs

Underline the subject(s) and verb(s) in each sentence in Form A. Mark each underlined word with "S" for subject or "V" for verb.

Activity C: Practicing with the information in Form A

1. How long did Edison go to school?
2. What did Edison like?
3. Could Edison hear well?
4. What did Edison look like?
5. What was Edison like?

Activity D: Adding information to the dictation

Where does the following information fit into Form A? Copy Form A, and add these pieces of information in logical places.

1. in 1931
2. from a childhood accident
3. creativity
4. and a square jaw
5. , especially science

Activity E: Practicing with adjective and noun forms

Here are some words that describe Edison's personality. Decide which word in each pair is a noun (N) and which is an adjective (ADJ). Follow the sentence patterns in the example, and write a sentence about Edison with each word.

1. a. (creative) *ADJ Edison was creative.*
   b. (creativity) *N Edison had remarkable creativity.*
2. a. (curiosity) ....
   b. (curious) ....
3. a. (determined) ....
   b. (determination) ....
4. a. (energetic) ....
   b. (energy) ....
5. a. (self-confidence) ....
   b. (self-confident) ....

Activity F: Matching

Here is some more interesting information about Edison. Match the words in the list with the sentences in the box.

a) energetic
b) creative
c) a good organizer
d) great determination
e) little formal education
f) remarkable
g) intense curiosity
h) practical

_____ 1. Edison asked questions constantly.
_____ 2. He worked on things that people wanted. He tried to make things that did not break easily, were easy to fix, and worked in ordinary conditions.
_____ 3. He organized the first industrial research lab. There, he directed teams of people in systematic research.
_____ 4. As a telegraph operator, Edison preferred the night shift because it gave him time for his experiments. He did not want an operation for his deafness. He said that silence helped his concentration.
_____ 5. He often did thousands of experiments to perfect an invention. For example, he did over 10,000 experiments to make a cheap battery for cars.
_____ 6. He went to school only three months.
_____ 7. Edison always worked very hard and seldom slept more than four hours a day.
_____ 8. He made over 1,000 inventions during his lifetime.

Activity G: Completing a paragraph

Put information about Edison into the framework below. Copy your paragraph on a clean sheet of paper. (NOTE: Most of the blanks require several words.)

Thomas Edison

Thomas Edison .... intensely curious and ....

constantly. He .... remarkable energy. He .... 4 hours a

day. He also .... remarkable determination. He ....

Edison .... a practical organizer who worked on .... and

organized the first .... He .... deaf, but did not want

.... deafness. He said .... concentration.

Activity H: Practicing for the dictation quiz on Form B

Study the structure and spelling in Form A. Make a cloze exercise with Form A. Omit every 3rd, 4th, or 5th word, as your teacher directs.

5.5 TALENTED TWINS: Practice text

Situation: Bill and Tom (p. 30) have twin friends named Lisa and Laura.

Activity A: Learning about Lisa and Laura

There are six pieces of information about Lisa and Laura in the box. Write one question about each piece of information. Work with a partner. Take turns asking and answering the questions.

1. When .... ?

2. Where .... ?

3. What .... ?

4. What .... ?

5. What .... like?

6. When .... ?

1. Date of birth: July, 1959
2. Place of birth: Albany, New York
3. Physical appearance:
   – hair: auburn
            wavy
   – eyes: hazel
            wideset
4. Personality and characteristics:
   – somewhat shy
   – dislike noisy parties
   – common sense
   – talented in music
5. Hobbies: all types of music
   ranging from classical to rock
   – Lisa: violin in the community
             orchestra
   – Laura: piano in a jazz group
6. Education
   – average students
   – major: English
   – degree: B.A. (1980)

Activity B: Making changes in paragraphs

Find the paragraph "Similar Siblings" in your notebook (see Activity A on page 30). Rewrite this paragraph with the information in the box. Change "Bill and Tom" to "Lisa and Laura." Use the title "Talented Twins."

5.6   DESCRIBING APPEARANCE AND PERSONALITY: Spider diagram

Activity A: Organizing vocabulary

These words answer the question, "What does s/he look like?" Put them in the spider diagram on page 94. You must sometimes decide whether a word applies only to men, only to women, or to both.

attractive	chubby	handsome	oval	slender
auburn	crooked	hazel	petite	slim
bald	curly	heavy	pimples (X)	stocky
bangs	dark (3)	long	pointed	straight
a beard	fair	a medium build	a ponytail	tall
beautiful	fat (X)	medium-height	pretty	thick
black (3)	freckles	medium-length	red	thin
blond	a good build	medium-weight	round	wavy
blue	a good figure	a moustache	salt-and-pepper	wide
braids	good-looking	muscular	short (2)	wide-set
brown (3)	gray	nice-looking	sideburns	wrinkles
a bun	green	ordinary-looking	skinny (X)	

(2) = use twice   (3) = use three times   (X) = impolite, even if true

Put a checkmark (√) beside thirteen nouns in the diagram that are used in this pattern:
S/he has . . . .
⫸→

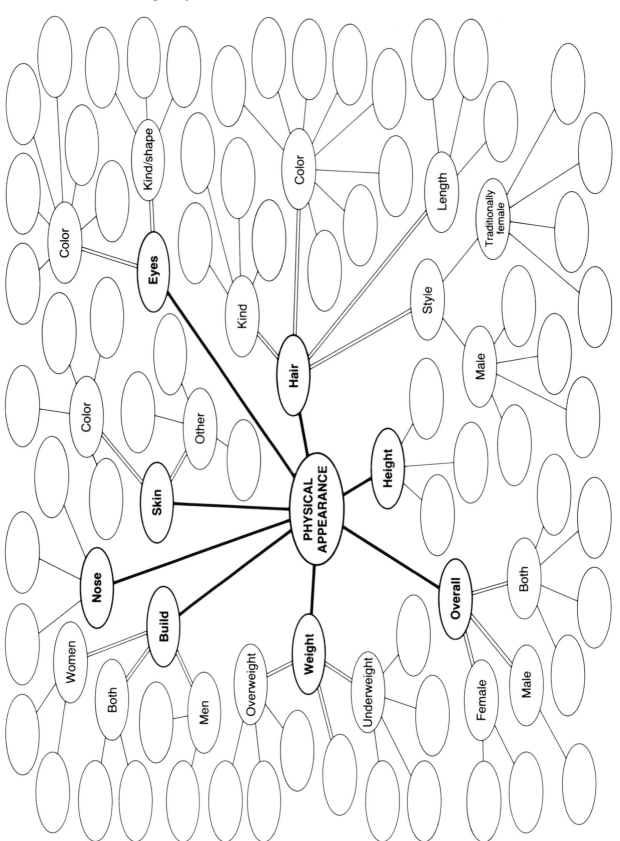

Activity B: Ordering adjectives in a series

You sometimes need two or three adjectives to describe someone's hair, eyes, beard, or other part of the body. Generally, you put the adjectives in this order:

S/he has (a/an) _____   _____   _____

length/size   kind/shape   (shade) color

| hair |
| eyes |
| eyebrows |
| eyelashes |
| beard |
| etc. |

Examples: She has short dark brown hair.
He has a long bushy black beard.
She has soft brown skin.

She has long hair. **NOT** *She has a long hair.*

Write each of the groups of words in the correct order on the corresponding blank lines. Add periods, question marks, and capital letters as needed.

1. round	2. he	3. black	4. nose	5. ponytails
has	eyebrows	have	auburn	medium-length
eyes	white	Tom	beard	twins
blue	does	Bill	big	dark
Betty	thick	eyelashes	grandpa	have
large	have	long	red	do
		and	a	blond
		curly	my	the
		both	an	
			and	
			has	

1. ....

....

2. ....

....

3. ....

....

4. ....

....

5. ....

....

⫸→

6. sideburns	7. father	8. braids	9. bangs	10. and
had	bald	your	a	grandmother
uncle	had	have	has	pointed
a	but	mother	Martha	had
thick	beard	did	long	hair
my	was	ever	and	a
black	short		bun	salt-and-pepper
moustache	my			my
gray	a			long
and	brown			nose

6. ....

....

7. ....

....

8. ....

....

9. ....

....

10. ....

....

Activity C: Matching opposites

These words are useful in answering the question, "What is s/he like?" Write each word in the list beside its opposite (antonym) in the box. Work with a partner or a small group. Match as many words as possible *before* using the dictionary.

cautious	immature	moody	serious
dishonest	impractical	not too bright	tactful
flexible	inconsiderate	optimistic	tolerant
grouchy	insecure	relaxed	undisciplined
hard-working	irresponsible	reserved	unselfish

blunt/ ....   lazy/ ....

cheerful/ ....   mature/ ....

confident/ ....   nervous/ ....

considerate/ ....   outgoing/ ....

critical/ ....   pessimistic/...........................

disciplined/ ....   practical/ ....

good-natured/ ....   responsible/ ....

honest/	selfish/ ....
impulsive/	stubborn/ ....
intelligent/	witty/ ....

5.7 *REVISING:* *Sylvia's self-portrait*

Sylvia wrote a paragraph about herself. She read it several times, but she wasn't happy with it. She rewrote it to make it better. Read her two paragraphs, and answer the questions.

1. How are the two paragraphs alike? ....
   ....

2. How are the paragraphs different? ....
   ....

3. Which paragraph is better? Why? ....
   ....

Box A

> ### Self-Portrait
>
> I am a practical, hard-working person. I am five feet seven inches tall and weigh 140 pounds. I have long wavy auburn hair. I sometimes have a ponytail, but only in the summer when I go swimming every day. I have light blue eyes, pale skin, and freckles. My nose is wide and flat. In general, I am an ordinary-looking person, except for my pretty hair.

Box B

> ### Self-Portrait
>
> I am a practical, hard-working person. I am five feet seven inches tall and weigh 140 pounds. My sister weighs 140 pounds, too. I have long wavy auburn hair. I sometimes have a ponytail, but only in the summer when I go swimming every day. Swimming is really fun. I have light blue eyes, pale skin, and freckles. In general, I am an ordinary-looking person, except for my pretty hair.

5.8 EDITING: Practice with symbols

Activity A: Finding editing problems

Cover the editing symbols. While you read the paragraph, put a checkmark (√) near each editing problem you find. Then uncover the symbols and compare them with your checks.

COVER↓

poss	My great-grandpa name was
ww	William Henry Langdon. Much people
VT	called him "Will," but I call him
	"Pappy." When he was in his twenties,
/	he had a curly brown hair, but by
ww, /	the age of 35 he had bald hair.
R(, Ⓥ	He was handsome and warm
WF, Ⓥ	blue eyes, he weight 200 lbs. and
⌐	tall 5 feet 9 inches. He was stocky
✗ , ⑤	and very strong, because worked
	hard on his farm every day. Pappy
ⓐⓡⓣ	was practical man. He never bought
ww, VT	nothing that he does not need.
( )ᶠ, VT	Also generous man. He always give
	money and food to poor people.
	Unfortunately he also got angry
WF, WF	easy. Pappy liked hunt.
ᶠ(, rep	Because it was fun and it was
)ᶠ	practical.

Activity B: Making corrections

Rewrite the paragraph in Activity A. Make all necessary changes. Use the editing symbols and your checks as a guide.

5.9   *DAN'S LEAST FAVORITE DAY: Practice text*

Activity A: Combining sentences

Rewrite the paragraph. Combine the sentences as indicated. Use each of these words one time: *and, but, or, because*. Omit the numbers.

a) Combine 2 and 3.
b) Combine 5 and 6.
c) Combine 7 and 8.
d) Combine 9 and 10.

Dan's Least Favorite Day

[1]Dan hates to do his laundry.   [2]He needs to wash his clothes every two weeks.   [3]He always waits three weeks until everything is dirty.   [4]He doesn't like to sort his clothes.   [5]He usually forgets to take detergent to the laundromat.   [6]He has to ask another customer for some of his.   [7]He often has to get change in the grocery store.   [8]The change machine in the laundromat seldom works.   [9]He doesn't like to fold his clothes.   [10]He doesn't like to put them on hangers.   [11]In fact, Dan dislikes everything about doing his laundry with one exception.   [12]He likes to finish!   [13]That's why he always says, "When I'm rich, I will never do my own laundry again!"

Activity B: Making changes in paragraphs

1. Dan is rich now, so he never has to do his laundry. Now, he sends it out. Write about Dan before he became rich. Omit the numbers. Your first sentence: "Before Dan got rich, he hated to do his laundry."

2. Lisa and Laura dislike doing their laundry, too. Write about them. Omit the numbers. Your first sentence: "Lisa and Laura hate to do their laundry."

5.10 ACTIVE VOCABULARY PRACTICE: Silent quizzes

Your teacher will call out a number and demonstrate an action *silently*. Find the action on the list. Beside it, write the number the teacher called out.

Silent Quiz I

____ bite	____ clap	____ sneeze
____ blink	____ laugh	____ tiptoe
____ catch	____ point	____ try to reach
____ chew	____ smile	____ wave

Silent Quiz II

____ bend	____ cry	____ throw
____ blow	____ frown	____ wave
____ climb	____ kick	____ wink
____ cough	____ shrug	____ yawn

Silent Quiz III

____ ankle	____ fist	____ shoulder
____ cheeks	____ knee	____ toes
____ chin	____ neck	____ waist
____ elbow	____ shin	____ wrist

5.11 FAMILY HISTORY PROJECT – PERSONAL DESCRIPTION: Composition

Activity A: Describing personality

1. List six adjectives that describe the personality of your family member. Include both good and bad parts of his or her personality.

a) ....

b) ....

c) ....

d) ....

e) ....

f) ....

2. Take turns with a partner. Choose one adjective from your list, but keep your choice *secret*. Explain this word to your partner, but *don't* say the word on your list. Instead, illustrate the word by giving examples from your family member's life. Then show your list and ask your partner to identify the adjective you talked about.

Example: a) lazy
               b) outgoing
               c) grouchy

You say, "Her house was always full of people, especially on the weekends. She often invited friends or relatives to come for dinner and a game of cards."

Activity B: Describing interests

1. List six things your family member liked to do.

a) ....

b) ....

c) ....

d) ....

e) ....

f) ....

2. Choose two activities from your list. Explain what your family member regularly did that showed that she or he liked these activities. Write two sentences about each, but don't use the words from the list in your sentences.

Example:

Cooking

She liked to prepare big, special meals for her family on all the holidays. Her kitchen was always full of homemade cookies for her visitors.

1) ....

....

....

....

2) ....

....

....

....

Activity C: Writing a description

Write a paragraph describing your family member. Tell about his or her personality, interests, and physical appearance. Use your ideas from Activities A and B as a starting point.

Unit 6   Describing People's Lives

(see Teachers' Notes on pp. 159–167)

6.1   HALEY'S FAMILY HISTORY PROJECT: *Dictation*

Activity A: Dictation

Write the paragraph as your teacher dictates. When you finish, compare what you wrote with Form A in the box.

> **Haley's Family History Project (Form A)**
>
> As a child, Alex Haley, an American author, learned a few African words from his grandmother. They had been in his family for seven generations. These words helped Haley discover the tribal origin of his great-great-great-great-grandfather, Kunta Kinte. In 1767 Kinte was kidnapped in western Africa, brought to America, and sold as a slave. Eventually, Haley wrote <u>Roots</u>, a historical novel that tells Kinte's story and the next 200 years of Haley's family history.

Activity B: Talking about the dictation

Part I. Practice with information in the dictation.

1. What was in Haley's family for seven generations?
2. Who taught the words to Haley?
3. Who was Kunta Kinte?
4. How did Kunta Kinte become a slave?
5. What was the name of Haley's book?

Part II. Practice with information related to the dictation.

6. What is a root? Why did Haley use this word as the title for his book?
7. When did slavery end in the United States? Which U.S. president ended slavery?

103

Activity C: Making changes in paragraphs

Rewrite Form A. Substitute these words and phrases for other words with the same or similar meaning.

1. six-year-old
2. ancestor
3. shipped across the Atlantic
4. following
5. after twelve years of research and writing
6. used both facts and his own imagination to complete

Activity D: Adding information

Rewrite Form A. Add the following items in their logical places.

1. in chains
2. on her front porch in Tennessee
3. moving
4. black
5. along with court records, census lists, and maritime documents
6. The book, published in 1976, became a best seller and was soon made into a twelve-part television drama.

Activity E: Preparing for the dictation quiz on Form B

Study the words and structures in Form A. Make a cloze exercise by omitting every 3rd, 4th, or 5th word, as your teacher directs.

6.2 REVISING: "Edison's Most Famous Invention"

Activity A: Getting information from a lecture

Read these questions. Then listen as your teacher reads a short lecture about Thomas Edison's most famous invention. Take as many notes as you can, and use your notes to answer the questions.

1. What is Thomas Edison's most famous invention? ....
....
2. What does this invention do? ....
....
3. When did Edison begin working on it? ....
4. What was Edison's first problem? ....
....

5. What was his second problem? ....

   ....

6. What are the names of these parts of Edison's invention?

   a. ....

   b. ....

   c. ....

7. What was the total amount of time Edison worked on this invention? ....

   ....

8. How long did Edison's first bulb last? ....

   How long do modern ones last? ....

*Edison with
movie projector*

Activity B: Working with a summary

In the box is Henry's first draft of a summary of the lecture about Edison's invention. Unfortunately, Henry didn't use his lecture notes while writing, so his summary has many factual mistakes and missing words. Read Henry's summary and help him begin to revise it.

1. Check the facts in the summary. Use your lecture notes from Activity A. Find and circle 15 FACTUAL mistakes in the summary.
2. Fill in the blanks in the summary with these words:

oxygen	filament	glows	electricity	carbonized thread
vacuum	melt	practical	through	bamboo

Henry's summary

Edison's Least Famous Invention

1   Edison's most famous invention is the electric light bulb. Edison began to

2   work on it in 1879 and did a few experiments during two years. His plan was to

3   change _____ into light by passing an electric

4   current through a thin piece of material. When electricity passes _____

5   a material, the material gets very cold. When this happens, the material

6   _____ brightly and makes light.

7   His first problem was _____ . When

8   it is present, materials burn easily. There is oxygen in air, so Edison

9   needed to keep water away from his materials. He made a metal bulb and

10   put his materials inside it. Then he took the air out of the bulb and made a

11   _____ inside it.

12   Edison's second and more difficult problem was to find the best material

13   for the _____ . He needed something that did not _____ ,

14   that glowed brightly, and that lasted a short time. He tried a few materials. He

15   even used a blond hair from a friend's beard. It worked well. He also used

16   platinum. The platinum filament worked, but not well, and it was very

17   inexpensive. Finally, he used a _____ . His filament of

18   carbonized thread worked! It was cheap and had a high melting point. Thus, in

19   1879, the first _____ electric light bulb was born. A year later,

20   with a filament of carbonized _____ , it was ready to sell.

21   Modern light bulbs are the same as Edison's first bulb. His lasted for only

22   four hours, but today's bulbs have an average life of more than 1,000 years.

23   Also, his bulb had a vacuum inside, but modern bulbs are filled with nitrogen

24   and oxygen.

Activity C: Revising the summary

On a clean sheet of paper, revise Henry's summary by recopying it and correcting the 15 factual mistakes you circled. Use your lecture notes from Activity A to make the corrections.

6.3 WORKING WITH A BIOGRAPHY: Edison

Activity A: Collecting biographical information

A biography is the story of a person's life. Look at your papers about Thomas Edison from this unit and Units 3 and 5 to find information about his life. Work with a partner or small group to complete the outline.

Facts about Edison's Life

A. Childhood
  1. Birth – Ohio – Feb. 11, ? _____
  2. Loved ? _____ – very good memory – ? _____ about science
  3. ? ____ mos. of formal educ. – trouble in school – mother became teacher

B. Adolescence
  1. 1859 – 1st job – selling newspapers + snacks on trains – accident made him ? _____
  2. printed own newspaper + had lab in baggage car – result: started fire + lost job
  3. 1862 – telegraph operator on night shift – made an invention to do his work – result: fired for sleeping

C. Important events in career
  1. 1869 – 1st patented invention – not wanted – result: worked on what people ? _____
  2. 1870 – 1st sale – stock price printer – $40,000 – result: opened lab + factory – Newark, New Jersey
  3. 1876 – world's 1st industrial ? _____ lab – Menlo Park, N.J. – teams of people – systematic research – 40 inventions at once – this organization perhaps = greatest invention

⟫→

D. __Important inventions__
  1. Many inventions, # = ? _____ ; examples: ? _____,
    motion-picture camera, cheap storage ? _____ for cars +
    streetcars
  2. improvements on telephone + telegraph
  3. most famous invention = 1st practical electric light ? _____
    in ? _____ ; filament = ? _____ thread – tested many
    materials, # = ? _____ – more than 1 year later: ready
    for sale

E. __Personal data__
  1. married twice – 5 children – son, Gov. of N.J.
  2. refused operation for ? _____ – said silence helped
    ? _____
  3. unusual daily routine – ? _____ hrs. of sleep per day
  4. genius = ? _____ % perspiration + ? _____ % inspiration
  5. death – Oct. 17, ? _____ – still working

Activity B: Completing a short biography

1. Compare the outline in Activity A with the biography of Edison.

   a) How many divisions are in the outline?
   b) How many paragraphs are in the biography?
   c) What is the topic of each paragraph?

2. Fill in the blanks in the biography of Edison. Use facts from the outline and your knowledge of English. Work with a partner or small group.

Edison: America's Most Famous _____

1   Thomas _____ Edison was born _____ Ohio _____

2 February 11, 1847. He loved books, had _____ excellent memory, and

3 showed curiosity about science, _____ he had trouble in school. After

4 only three months of formal _____ , he left school and

5 _____ at home with his mother.

6   When Edison was only _____ years old, he began working.

7 First, he _____ newspapers and snacks on trains. One day, someone

8   grabbed his ears to pull him on a moving train, and he became almost

9   _____. Later, he printed his own newspaper and _____

10   experiments in the baggage car of a train. He lost this job _____

11   an experiment started a fire on the train. Next, at the age of _____ ,

12   Edison worked as a telegraph operator. He _____

13   the night shift because he had time for his experiments. He lost this job

14   _____ he was _____ while a new invention

15   did his work.

16   _____ 1869, Edison got his _____ patent on an invention, but

17   no one wanted it. After _____ , he worked on things people wanted.

18   In 1870, he finally _____ an invention for $40,000. He immediately

19   used this _____ to open a lab and factory in Newark, New Jersey.

20   _____ years later, in Menlo Park, _____ _____ ,

21   Edison opened the world's first _____ research lab.

22   There, he directed teams of people in systematic research on 40 inventions

23   at _____ time. Today some people think this organization was Edison's

24   _____ invention.

25   During his _____ Edison made more than _____

26   inventions, including the _____ , the motion-picture

27   camera, and a cheap storage battery _____ automobiles and streetcars.

28   He also _____ the telephone and telegraph. But his most

29   famous invention changed _____ into light. He

30   experimented with thousands of materials. In _____ , he passed an

31   electric current through a _____ of carbonized thread and

32   the first _____ electric light bulb was born. After

33   one more _____ of work, it was finally ready to sell.

34   Edison had a remarkable life. He married _____ times, and one

35   of his five children became Governor of New Jersey. Edison never had an

36   operation for his _____ . He _____ that silence

37   helped his concentration. He always worked very hard and _____

38   slept more than _____ hours a day. He believed that _____

39   was 99% perspiration and 1% inspiration. He was probably right. His eighty-

40   four _____ of energy and creativity changed the world. When he

41   _____ on October 17, _____ , he was still _____

42   on new ideas.

6.4 PERSONALITY PROFILE: Composition/newspaper activity

Activity A: Preparing questions for an interview

Here are some questions you can ask when you interview people about their lives. Complete the questions by filling in the blanks.

Childhood

1. What .... full name?

2. When and where .... born?

3. What ....
mother
father
   do?

4. How many brothers and sisters .... have?

   .... the oldest, the youngest, in the middle?

5. Where .... grow up?

6. What .... interested in when ....
   a child?

Education

7.
Where
When
   .... go to high school?

8.
Where
When
   .... college as
   an undergraduate?

   What .... major?

   When .... graduate?

9.
Where
When
   .... go to graduate school?

   In what field .... do your graduate work?

   What degree did you............?

Career

10. What jobs .... had and when?

11. What .... present job?

    How long .... had it?

12. What .... like about your present job?

    What .... dislike about it?

13. Why .... choose this career?

14. What .... professional goals for the future?

Personal information

15. How long .... lived here?

    .... lived in another country?

16. .... married?

    (............... .... children?)

17. What .... like to do in your leisure time?

18. What .... like best about yourself?

    What .... like to change about yourself?

19. In general, what .... your philosophy of life?

20. What .... your personal goals for the future?

Activity B: Practicing with the questions

Do a practice interview. Ask your teacher the questions you prepared in Activity A. Take careful notes of the answers.

Activity C: Interviewing a visitor

Your teacher will invite a visitor to your class. Use the questions from Activity A to interview this visitor. Take turns asking questions. Take careful notes of the answers. Use the notes to write a "Personality Profile" article for the class newspaper.

6.5   *PROFESSIONAL PROFILE: Practice text*

Activity A: Adding verbs

Fill in the blanks with the correct tenses of the verbs in this list. Use each verb at least one time.

attend	earn	have
be	enjoy	intend
become	enter	work

Situation: During Career Week, students at Midburg High School did interviews for a project called "Professional Profiles." Here is one of their reports.

Professional Profile: Charlotte Kyler

Charlotte Kyler (1) .... over twenty-two years of experience in banking. She (2) .... currently a loan officer at the Midburg National Bank where she (3) .... for seventeen years. Ms. Kyler (4) .... interested in a banking career at the age of sixteen while she (5) .... part-time in a bank during her summer vacation. She (6) .... Middle State University and (7) .... both graduate and undergraduate degrees in finance. Her first job (8) .... at Community State Bank where she (9) .... for five years. Ms. Kyler (10) .... on the city council since 1982 and (11) .... to run for mayor in the next election. In her leisure time she (12) .... jogging and hiking and often (13) .... local races. A native of Faraway, Montana, Ms. Kyler (14) .... married to architect Cranston Davis. They (15) .... two sons, who (16) .... Middle State University.

Activity B: Making changes in paragraphs

Unfortunately, Charlotte Kyler died in a car accident two days after the interview. Rewrite the paragraph with the necessary changes. Begin with "The late Charlotte Kyler. . . ."

6.6   *ACTIVE VOCABULARY PRACTICE:*   *Verb review*

Directions: Choose items from the list to complete the answers to the questions below. In Exercises A and B together, you can use every item at least one time. (Some questions have more than one answer.)

blink	kick	snap my fingers
blow a bubble	laugh	sneeze
bite my nails	make a fist	throw
catch	point	tickle his/her ribs
clap	raise my hand	tiptoe
cough	rub on lotion	whisper
cry	scratch	whistle
dial	shake hands	wink
draw a heart	shrug my shoulders	yawn
frown	slap it	

What do you do when......?   I ....

Exercise A

1. . . . you have a cold   1 . . . .

2. . . . you are sleepy   2 . . . .

3. . . . a mosquito bites you   3 . . . .

4. . . . you are going to spend all day at the beach   4 . . . .

5. . . . you want to ask a question in class   5 . . . .

6. . . . you don't know an answer   6 . . . .

7. . . . the baby is sleeping   7 . . . .

8. . . . the sun is in your eyes   8 . . . .

9. . . . you hear something funny   9 . . . .

10. . . . you liked the concert   10 . . . .

11. . . . you are nervous   11 . . . .

12. . . . you are teasing   12 . . . .

Exercise B

1. . . . you are angry   1 . . . .

2. . . . you are unhappy   2 . . . .

⇛→

3. ...you want to tell a secret 3 ....
4. ...you play soccer 4 ....
5. ...you play baseball 5 ....
6. ...you meet someone for the first time 6 ....
7. ...you are chewing bubble gum 7 ....
8. ...you give directions 8 ....
9. ...you are keeping time with the music 9 ....
10. ...you want to make someone laugh 10 ....
11. ...you are making a phone call 11 ....
12. ...you are making a valentine 12 ....

6.7 FAMILY HISTORY PROJECT – SIGNIFICANT EVENT: Composition

Activity A: Talking about a significant event

1. Choose one important event from your family member's life.
2. Work with a partner. Tell your partner about the significant event you chose. Make sure your partner can answer these questions:
   - What year did the event happen?
   - Where did it happen?
   - How old was your family member then?
   - What happened?
   - Why was this event significant in the person's life?

Activity B: Writing and reading about the event

1. Write about the significant event. Use the past tense. Make sure your paper answers the questions in Activity A.
2. Exchange papers with the same partner that you talked to in Activity A. Read your partner's paper. Tell your partner about anything that is not clear. Also, tell your partner about any additions that are needed.
3. Rewrite your paper. Make the changes and additions that your partner suggested.

Activity C: Editing papers

1. Read your partner's paper carefully. Underline all the verbs.
2. Reread the paper. Look for verb problems. Circle any verbs that are incorrect in any way. Remember that the event took place in the *past*.

3. Explain to your partner all the problems in his or her paper that you find.

4. Rewrite your own paper. Correct all types of problems you and your partner found. Make sure to correct all verb problems.

6.8   *FAMILY HISTORY PROJECT – SHORT BIOGRAPHY: Composition*

Activity A: Making an outline for a biography

Work with a partner or small group. Put each piece of information in this list under one of the four headings in the box. Then put the items under each heading in a logical order. Copy the finished outline on a clean sheet of paper.

> A. Childhood and early years
> B. Adulthood
> C. Older years
> D. Personal information

activities as a teenager
childhood interests
community service activities
date & place of birth
date of marriage; spouse's name; ages at marriage
date, place, & cause of death
education outside school
first job
health; health problems
hometown as an adult
hometown as a child
important event(s) in later years
languages and travel
lifelong interests
military service
# of brothers & sisters; order of birth
# of sons & daughters
# of years of education; graduation & major
    occupation(s); events in career
parents' names, occupations & economic status
personality traits (strengths & weaknesses)
philosophy of life; famous quotations
physical appearance as a young adult
religion
residence during older years
retirement date & activities
significant event(s) during adulthood
significant event(s) during childhood

Activity B: Outlining your family member's life

Begin with the outline from Activity A. Add, omit, or change the place or order of information to fit your family member's life. Beside each item in this new outline, write specific facts about your family member. Use information from your "Family History Fact Sheet" on page 42. (NOTE: "Facts about Edison's Life" on pages 107–8 is an example of how your finished outline will look.)

Activity C: Writing a biography

Write a short biography of your family member. Use the outline you made in Activity B as a guide.

6.9 *FAMILY HISTORY PROJECT – FINAL PAPER:* Composition

Activity A: Reviewing your papers

In addition to the short biography, you have five other papers about your family member. Find and reread these papers:

a) first thoughts   d) a personal description
b) typical daily routine   e) a significant event
c) an important place

Activity B: Organizing the parts

1. To finish your family history project, you will integrate your shorter papers with the biography to make *one* longer final paper for your future reader. Here is a diagram of the basic organization of the final paper, and one person's plan for integrating all of his papers.

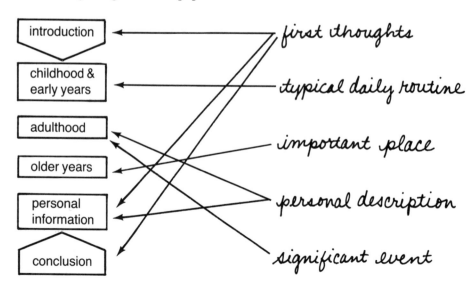

2. On a clean sheet of paper, draw a diagram of the basic organization of the final paper and *your* plan of integration.

Activity C: Writing the final paper

Write your final paper. Follow the plan you drew in Activity B.

Teachers' Notes

Unit 1   Getting Started

Important: If at all possible, remove, mask, or otherwise conceal pages 176–178 at the back of each student's book right away. In the Special Activities for story writing in the Teachers' Notes to Units 5 and 6, students will use the pictures on these pages but should be totally unfamiliar with them beforehand. If you can, cut out and file the pictures yourself before students receive their books. Otherwise it works well to bring scissors and stapler to class and have students cut the pages out of their own books. If the pictures are concealed in the first week of class, they will have faded sufficiently from the students' memory to preserve the information gaps necessary later on.

1.1   LETTERS ABOUT PEOPLE: *Practice text*   (p. 2)

Overview   This section contains classwork and homework for the first class session and will provide you with a brief introduction to your students' interests, goals, personalities, styles of participation, and writing abilities. Even if your students have already met each other, they can still benefit from this introduction to the conventions of informal, friendly letters. "Meet My Class," Section 2.1 in Unit 2, offers additional get-acquainted activities that can help you pull the class together later if membership has shifted due to late enrollment or class/level changes.

Before class   (1) Examine the question cues in Activity A, and adapt them as necessary to suit your situation. (2) Get a supply of unlined paper to give students for their letters to promote the idea that it is best to write letters on unlined paper.

In class   For Activity A try to pair students who do not know each other, instead of relying on chance or a student-chosen seating arrangement. Help students do Activity B orally, but assign actual writing of the letter as homework and move directly to Activity C.

Introduce Activity C by eliciting the following points. Similarity: The content of the framework is similar to the content of the second paragraph of the Activity B letter. Differences: This framework requires sentences with "I" and "my" rather than "he, his, she, her." (Have students practice making these changes orally.) It also introduces telephone number and mailing address. (Substitute local terminology for "zip code" and "area code" where necessary.) It lacks a date, salutation, and closing. (The salutation and closing must be appropriate for a letter to one's teacher. A comma, not a colon, is used after the salutation because this is also a friendly letter rather than a business one.)

After the discussion, hand out the unlined paper and have students write their letters in class. Since some students will finish ahead of others, plan some "buffer work" to occupy the fast finishers until everyone else is ready for the next activity. Easy, appropriate buffer work in this first class session is the previously previewed Activity B homework. When everyone has finished the Activity C letter, collect and save the letters for future reference because telephone numbers and addresses often come in handy. Remember to have any late-enrolling students write this letter, too.

1.2 THE BANK ROBBERY: *Picture composition* (p. 5)

In class Before discussing the pictures or doing any of the activities, get a *writing sample* from your students. To do this, have them look at the pictures on page 4 and write the story as well as they can on any paper and in any format they choose. Explain that you need to see what they can do. Reassure and encourage. After ten to fifteen minutes, collect the papers whether or not all students have finished. When you read these writing samples, do not mark them. Instead, use them to verify or adjust placement and form a first impression of each student's writing proficiency. Save the papers, and at the end of the course have students write the story again. You (and the students) can compare the two efforts to assess progress. Remember to have latecomers do this writing sample so they will have beginning markers, too.

As soon as you have collected the writing samples, have students look at the pictures and listen while you read aloud the whole story, using the script in Figure 1. Introduce Activity A orally by reading the first three or four sentences and asking students to tell the number of the corresponding picture. Then have them finish Activity A independently. Activities B and C may be done in class or as homework, but you should complete "Revising: Format," Section 1.3 of this unit, before assigning Activity C.

The Bank Robbery

A woman and her grandson are in the bank. The woman is making a deposit and cashing a check. Her handbag and her umbrella are on her arm. The boy has a balloon on a string. A man with a hat is walking in. His picture is on the bulletin board. The man walks to a window. He pulls out a gun. He shows a note that asks for money. He takes two bags of money. He starts to run away. The lady hits him with her umbrella. She stops him. A policeman takes the robber away. A crowd watches. The bank director gives the woman a reward. She looks happy to get the money. Her grandson also has a smile on his face. He gets seven balloons from the bank director.

Figure 1

1.3 REVISING: *Format* (p. 6)

Overview A superficial but necessary step in writing a paper is to make it *look* good. Point out that the format required in one culture – for example, signature at the end of the paper – may not be acceptable in another. The writing sample usually yields papers that you can use to demonstrate what is *not* appropriate.

In class With students' books closed, show students a piece of looseleaf notebook paper that you have labeled with a marker as shown in Figure 2. Tell them the names of the numbered parts. Then practice orally. You name a part, such as "top line," and have students tell you the number of the part. When students are proficient with the vocabulary, have them open their books and do Activities A and B. Here are some possible answers to Activity B: paper torn from spiral notebook, no title, no blank line, incorrect left-hand margin, no right-hand margin, name in wrong place, incorrect use of signature, indentations not the same size, indentations in the wrong places.

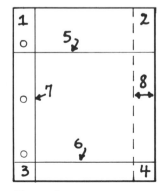

Figure 2

1.4 AN UNSUCCESSFUL CRIME: *Practice text*   (p. 8)

Before class   Make a display of the basic story text in Activity A. To make a display text, either put the text on an overhead projector transparency or copy it with bright markers on one or more pieces of big paper. Wrapping paper, butcher paper, and newsprint are all inexpensive and work well. Masking tape is an ideal adhesive because you can remove it easily from walls and paper. Then your display text can be folded, stored in a large envelope, folder, or bag, and reused several times.

A display text is indispensable in focusing everyone's attention on the same place in the story at the same time. Also, classwork seems more interesting when whole-class work with a display text alternates with individual work with the book. Even though the text in the book and the display text are identical, the dynamics of the two situations are different and worth cultivating.

Activity A   (1) Begin Activity A with students' books closed. Write "she" and "her" on the board. Ask students to listen carefully and count how many times they hear each word while you read the text aloud. Use the text in Figure 1 as a script. Repeat with "he" and "his." (Answers: she – 2; her – 6; he – 5; his – 2.) (2) Show students the display text, and read the story aloud again, sentence by sentence. As you read, fill in the missing verbs orally, but pause at each triangle and call on volunteers to supply the appropriate pronouns. (3) Have students open their books and write these pronouns in part 1 of Activity A. Check orally. (4) Refer to the display text again, and have students close their books. Call on volunteers to read one sentence and fill in the missing verb (as well as pronouns, where appropriate). (5) Have students open their books and work in pairs to write the missing verbs in part 2 of Activity A. Check with the whole class by writing the verbs on the board so students can check their spelling. Be sure to erase before proceeding. (6) Have students work with the same (or a different) partner and practice reading the entire story orally, according to the directions in part 3 of Activity A. Circulate and listen. (7) Finally, refer students back to the display text and have them close their books. Lead the class in an oral "chain" drill. To do this, have student 1 read sentence 1 of the story; student 2 read sentences 1 and 2; student 3 read sentences 1, 2, and 3, and so on. Students usually perceive the chain drill as a game. By the end, several students are usually eager to try reading the whole story.

Activities B, C, and D   Each of these writing activities requires students to produce a new version of the original story, by making certain changes in the story text from Activity A. Although the following procedure is applicable to all three activities and the activities can be done in any order, you should work with only one activity at any given class session.

Introduce each activity orally with students' books closed. Using the display text, explain how the story needs to be changed. Then read the first sentence aloud, making changes as you read. Ask volunteers to try to make similar changes in the next few sentences. When you think everyone understands the process, pair students and have them open their books and take turns reading the sentences and making the changes orally. Be sure to have them put away all pens and pencils so they won't be tempted to write instead of talk. Circulate and listen. When most pairs have finished, bring the class back together to practice orally with the display text one more time. Then assign the activity as written homework. After you have collected this homework, have the class warm up and review by doing the activity again, orally and as fluently as possible from the display text.

You may wish to save one of these activities to use as a test, as buffer work for fast finishers, or as review homework one, two, or even three weeks later. If you use the activities at intervals, students will build confidence and control through familiarity without getting bored.

Follow-up   The following activities, which do not appear in the student pages, can be used for warm-up, extension, or reinforcement anytime after Activity A.

(1) *Following directions and matching.* Ask students to take a piece of notebook paper, write their names in the upper left-hand corner, put the title "The Bank Robbery" on the top line, leave a blank space, and number from 1 to 9, skipping every other line. (Note that these directions reinforce vocabulary about format.) Dictate the questions in Figure 3 (p. 122) to be written beside the numbers. Then display the answers in Figure 3 either on a transparency or on big paper. Have students write each answer on the line below its corresponding question.

(2) *Writing Wh-questions and appropriate answers.* Collect magazine pictures that show actions, people, and situations, or ask students to

---

Questions

1. Whose picture was on the bulletin board?
2. Where did the bank robber go?
3. What did the bank robber pull out?
4. How much money did the bank robber take?
5. Who stopped the bank robber?
6. When did the policeman come?
7. Why was the little boy happy?
8. How many balloons did the little boy finally have?
9. Which person was smoking?

Answers (in random order)

the old lady, two bags, the bank robber's, the bank robber, eight, a little later, to the teller's window, because he got some new balloons, a gun.

Figure 3

bring them in. Give each pair of students a picture, or let students choose one if you have a large supply. Have each pair write nine questions and appropriate answers about their picture, one question with each of these words: who, what, where, when, why, how many, how much, which, and whose. Some of the questions may require a little imagination. If you have any fast finishers, put them in groups of four to ask each other the questions about their pictures. Collect the papers with the pictures for correction.

(3) *Writing and dramatizing a script.* Ask students to count and name the characters in the bank robbery story. Form groups to write a script and dramatize the story, with the requirement that each person must speak at least twice.

1.5   *LETTERS ABOUT THE BANK ROBBERY: Writing from a point of view*   (p. 10)

Activity A   Students enjoy this activity because it asks them to use their imagination. Discuss the letters one at a time. After students have fully explored a character's feelings, elicit ideas for opening sentences of the character's letter. Help students agree on a good opening, and write their first two sentences on the board for future reference. Continue until the first sentences of all four letters are on the board. Your class's letters may take a completely different direction, but here are the openings that one class came up with:

(1) Dear Fred,
    A crazy thing happened to me. I can't believe it. Yesterday I went to the bank. I was making a deposit. . . .
(2) Dear Martha,
    A terrible thing happened to me! I can't believe it. Yesterday I was working. A robber pulled out a gun. . . .
(3) Dear Mr. Wilson:
    The cost of living is high. I had no money. . . .

(4) Dear Officer Reed:
    Yesterday I was in the bank when a man came in and . . . .

Activity B   (1) Point out to students that two different punctuation marks are used with salutations. Have them look at the salutations with a colon and decide whether this type of salutation is used for friendly letters or business letters. After they understand that salutations with a colon are used for business letters, ask them to identify the business letters (#3 and #4) in Activity A and decide which of the salutations with a colon would be appropriate for a lawyer and a police officer. As they match salutations with letters, write each salutation on the board above the opening sentences of that letter. Repeat this process by having them match the salutations with commas to one or the other of the friendly letters (#1 and #2) in Activity A. (Note that the sample opening sentences of each letter, shown above, are preceded by an appropriate salutation.)

(2) Have students look at the closings, and help them decide which are for friendly letters (Love, Warmly, Fondly) and which are for business letters (Sincerely, Very truly yours, Yours sincerely). Point out that all closings are followed by a comma. Then ask students to choose one appropriate closing for each letter, and write their choice on the board below each letter.

Activity C   Pair students, or form small groups of three or four students, to collaborate on finishing one of the letters. Either assign a letter to each group or allow the groups to choose, but make sure that each letter is done by at least one group.

If you have a fast-finishing group, have one member of the group read the letter aloud to you. Then, for buffer work, have the group add a "real-life" closing paragraph, with remarks and questions about family, having little time to write, upcoming vacation, jail routine, and so on, while the other groups are finishing. In some classes, you may want all of the groups to add such a paragraph.

When all groups have finished the basic letter, bring the class together to listen to a student from each group read its letter. Then collect the letters. Underline the major errors, and make suggestions for additional sentences where necessary. Return the letters to the groups. Ask students to work together on changes, but have each student write an individual copy of the letter to be turned in for a final check.

1.6 *ACTIVE VOCABULARY PRACTICE:*   *Basic classroom stretch*   (p. 11)

Overview   Active Vocabulary Practice (AVP) exercises are inspired by Total Physical Response (TPR), a procedure advocated and tested by James Asher. Asher showed that students acquire and retain vocabulary with significantly enhanced efficiency when they physically act out verbal commands but are not pressured to say the words. These AVP exercises (1) expand common vocabulary, (2) preview or reinforce vocabulary students meet in other activities, (3) improve ability to follow directions, and (4) provide an enjoyable change from paper and pencil work.

All the AVP exercises in this book are appropriate in North America for males and females of all ages. The appropriateness of some actions does, however, vary from culture to culture according to age, sex or situation; for example, in general Chinese women do not whistle. If and when your students point out such variations, welcome their comments and use them nonjudgmentally to elicit discussion of cultural differences.

Exercise A

Before class   Copy the exercises on small cue cards, which you can eventually file in an envelope for repeated use and review. Add vocabulary for other objects found in your classroom. These cue cards will prompt your memory and allow you to demonstrate the actions unencumbered by the book.

In class   Do the exercises between two major activities and after students have been sitting for a while. Or, do them five minutes before a break or the end of class when students mentally tune out anything that is not light and quick. About five minutes of AVP per class session is sufficient.

Do the exercises with books closed. Give the commands and act them out with the students. Keep a brisk pace. When you feel that students have mastered a given command, give the command but do not act. After students have acted (or not acted), demonstrate the correct response. Conduct the exercises with a sense of humor and a willingness to poke a little fun at yourself. Use "hammy," exaggerated facial expressions and gestures to set an informal tone and put everyone at ease.

(Repeat and mix commands in response to students' progress.)
Stand up. / Stretch. / Touch your toes. / Touch your nose. / Touch your hair. / Touch your right eye. / Touch your left eye. / Touch both knees. / Touch only your left knee. / Touch only your right knee. / Stretch. / Sit down. / Stand up. / Shake hands with another person. / Sit down. / (Or, if the class is going to take a break or end for the day:) Wave good-bye.

Exercise B

Stand up. / Stretch. / Wave hello and shake hands. / Touch your toes (nose, hair, head, left eye, right eye, both eyes, right shoulder, left shoulder, both shoulders, both ears, knees). / Point to the door (window, blackboard, clock, eraser, wastebasket, bulletin board, ceiling, floor, light). / Point to your right elbow. / Touch your right elbow. / Point up (down, to the left, to the right, to the teacher, to Joe). / Touch both ears. / Point to your right ear. / Touch your right ear. / Shake hands with another student. / Sit down.

Exercise C

Stand up. / Stretch. / Touch your head (shoulders, knees, elbows, ankles, toes). / Point to your chin (mouth, teeth). / Point to the bulletin board. / Point to the upper (lower, left-hand, right-hand) corner of the blackboard. / Walk forward. Stop! / Walk backward. Stop! / Smile. / Laugh. / Frown. / Make a fist. / Shake your fist. / Shake hands with someone else. / Shake your left arm. / Shake your right foot. / Listen to your watch. Frown. Hit your watch. / Frown (you forgot something). Hit your forehead. / Open your eyes wide. Open your mouth. Look surprised. Hit your cheek with the palm of your hand. / Wave good-bye. / Sit down.

Exercise D

(This one is a seated activity. To monitor it, keep an eye on as many of your students' papers and faces as possible. After you give a command two or three times, demonstrate it so students can check what they have done.)

Take out a piece of paper and a pencil or a pen. / Number from 1 to 8 along the left margin. / Write "Wednesday" beside number 4. / Underline number 7. / Circle number 6. / Sign your name in the lower left-hand corner. / Draw a house in the upper right-hand corner. / Cross out number 3. / Write "June" beside number 5. / Draw a line through "June." / Fold your paper into thirds.

Follow-up   As the students (and you) become proficient, mix, review, and vary the exercises, and create your own sequences. Feel free to move on to the AVP exercises in Unit 2 if your students are ready for them before you finish the other activities in this unit.

1.7 EXERCISE FOR BUSY PEOPLE: *Practice text*   (p. 12)

In class   (1) Introduce the topic of exercise by referring to the Active Vocabulary Practice exercises the class has been doing. Write questions about exercise on the board, and have students work in pairs to ask each other the questions and report their answers to the class. For variety, have everyone stand during this activity.

1. What activities are good exercise?
2. Why do people exercise?
3. Do you like to exercise?
4. What type of exercise do you do?
5. How often should a person exercise?
6. How often do you exercise?

(2) Continue preparation for the practice text by doing a listening comprehension exercise, for which materials are given in Figure 4, to focus attention on the overall content of the combined paragraph before concentrating on sentence-by-sentence

Today John Jones, a typical worker, has a job inside a tall building or modern factory. He spends eight busy hours at work but rarely uses his muscles. He exercises only on sunny weekends at a nearby park. A worker such as John needs to get regular exercise. Here are two people who know easy ways to do this. An important lawyer walks to work every day. She wears an expensive suit and old jogging shoes. She carries her nice shoes in her briefcase. An employee of a big factory takes short breaks in the morning and afternoon. He stretches and touches his toes beside a huge machine. Exercise is important to this man and woman because it makes them feel better.

1. Who works in a tall building or modern factory?
2. Who walks to work every day?
3. Who takes short breaks every morning and afternoon?
4. When does the typical worker exercise?
5. What does the lawyer wear to work?
6. Where does the factory employee exercise?

Figure 4

manipulation. Mastery of content is not required, however, so do not linger even if students have some difficulty with the exercise. The incidental exposure to the combined paragraph is what counts.

Figure 4 contains the practice text in combined form and six comprehension questions about it. With students' books still closed, dictate the first three questions for students to write on scrap paper. Then read the combined paragraph aloud one or two times, and have students listen for short answers to the questions. Check their answers orally, and then dictate the last three questions. Reread the combined paragraph once or twice more while students listen again for short answers. Check orally.

(3) Begin Activity A by having students put away their pens and pencils. Work through all or part of the activity orally. Then, prompted by students, begin writing (or have a student begin writing) the combined paragraph on the board. Have students copy this first part from the board and finish the paragraph for homework. At the next class session, after collecting the homework, do the activity again orally. Activity B, which requires a change from singular to plural, may be done at any time after you have returned the Activity A homework. Again, begin the activity orally before assigning it as written work.

Follow-up   (1) After students have learned how to make a cloze exercise (page 14), ask one student (a fast finisher or someone in need of a little limelight) to write the finished paragraph from Activity A or B as a cloze exercise. Duplicate the cloze, and use it as homework or buffer work for fast finishers.

(2) Save (or have students save) the finished paragraphs for students to mark for additional practice after they have completed Section 1.9, "Editing: Subjects and verbs."

1.8 REASONS FOR EXERCISING: *Dictation* (p. 13)

Overview   In both educational and everyday situations people are expected to write down accurately language they have never heard before. Dictations help students develop the ability to do this and provide a relatively painless way to improve spelling and handwriting, learn new vocabulary, and find out information about a variety of new topics.

In this and every unit, the dictation activities will require part of at least four class sessions. The general lesson plan that follows is applicable to all six dictations in the book. For each dictation there are two forms: *Form A* (given in Activity A in the student pages) and *Form B* (given in the Teachers' Notes). Form A is used for all the activities in the student pages. Form B is used as a dictation quiz to be given after students have done all the activities with Form A. Form B is a variation of Form A and uses the same words in a different order to convey the same ideas as Form A.   ⟫→

INSTRUCTIONS FOR ADMINISTRATION OF FORM A AND FORM B

1. LISTEN ONLY. DO NOT WRITE. (Read the text at near-native speed.)

> Reasons for Exercising (Form A)
>
> Why does a person / exercise? / Some people exercise / for their cardiovascular health. / Other people exercise / to burn calories / and lose weight. / They want / to look better. / Still others exercise / for fun and relaxation. / In fact, / most people probably exercise / for all three reasons.

2. LISTEN AND WRITE. (Read the text in phrases as marked, pausing between phrases for students to write. Adjust the length of the phrases to fit your students' proficiency. Read each phrase no more than twice.)

3. YOU HAVE ONE MINUTE TO STUDY YOUR WORK. (Adjust time as necessary depending on the length of the text and proficiency of your students.)

4. LISTEN AGAIN, AND CHECK YOUR WORK. (Read the text at a slow but natural speed. Read complete sentences, pausing only slightly in between.)

Figure 5

Before class   If equipment is available, record both Form A and Form B of the dictation on tape, according to the instructions in Figure 5, for use in place of "live" dictation.

Day 1: Form A and associated activities   (1) With students' books closed, begin Activity A by dictating Form A to students, according to the instructions in Figure 5. (Do *not* assign Form A for study beforehand.) When students have finished checking their work, have them open their books, compare their work with Form A in Activity A, and circle all errors, omissions, and additions. Collect these papers to motivate students and monitor progress. (2) Then ask the discussion questions in Activity B in an informal, conversational fashion. Have students use whatever dictionaries, reference books, or outside people are available to answer any "difficult" questions. (3) Introduce Activity C, which requires students to expand Form A. It may be done orally or in writing, at home or in class. Students find it both thought-provoking and enjoyable. (4) For homework, have students write a cloze exercise based on Form A, as shown in Activity D. Making this cloze is good preparation for the Form B quiz on Day 3. Have students begin writing their clozes in class to make sure they understand what to do. Here are some additional ideas for the clozes:

– To facilitate sharing the clozes on Day 2, have half of the students omit every 5th word and the other half omit every 6th word.
– For more challenging clozes, have students omit every 3rd or 4th word.
– With strong classes, have students prepare cloze exercises based on the expanded version of Form A from Activity C.

Day 2: Cloze and Form A practice   Have students exchange their cloze homework exercises, preferably with someone who has omitted words by a different system. Have students fold up the bottom of their classmate's paper in accordion fashion to cover the answers, as shown in Figure 6,

Figure 6

and work through the cloze, writing answers at the bottom of the page. They can check their work by unfolding the paper. This sharing procedure not only motivates students to do the homework and do it well, but also gives additional practice with the text. Then choose one or more of the following options for 5 to 10 more minutes of practice.

1. Choose some of the more difficult words from Form A, and dictate them one at a time.
2. Do the following "here's-the-answer-now-write-the-question" activity. Dictate a few short sentences, such as the ones shown below, which are based on the text and contain key words. After students have written all the sentences, give them a Wh-word for each sentence. Have students use the given word to write a Wh-question that the dictated sentence answers. Collect the students' work, ask some of their questions orally, and call on volunteers to answer orally. Correct and return the papers. Here are some sample sentences and Wh-words for this dictation.
   a) People exercise for many reasons. (Why?)
   b) Exercise burns calories. (What?)
   c) Some people relax by exercising. (How?)
3. Dictate Form A again, using a tape-recorded version if possible. Have students work in small groups or as a whole class.

Day 3: Dictation quiz with Form B   Dictate Form B of the dictation, shown below, as a quiz. With abler classes, you can make the quiz more difficult by expanding Form B to include the words in Activity C. Use the instructions in Figure 5. Collect the papers, and immediately display Form B on a transparency or big paper so that students can evaluate their performance.

Form B   Why do most people exercise? Most people exercise for three reasons. They exercise for relaxation and fun. They exercise for their cardiovascular health, and they exercise to lose weight and look better. (32 words)

Day 4: Returning graded quizzes   Return the quizzes with errors, omissions, additions, and format mistakes circled but not corrected. Overall grades can be calculated by subtracting, in this case, 3 points per circle from 100. Display Form B again so that students can fill in missing words and make other corrections. Or, group students and have them work together to produce a perfect copy of Form B. If students perform poorly on the quiz, you can create your own variation of the dictation – call it Form C – and dictate it as a second quiz at the next class session.

1.9   EDITING: *Subjects and verbs*   (p. 15)

Overview   The "editing" activities in each unit prepare students for correction of written work, particularly the second drafts of their compositions. Appendix 2 contains a complete list of the editing symbols used in this book.

In class   With students' books closed, write on the board several sentences lacking a subject or a verb. Collect such sentences from student papers. The writing sample from Section 1.2, "The Bank Robbery," is a good source. Try to elicit

suggestions for correction and some statement of the problem before starting activities in the book.

Follow-up   (1) After students have completed Activities A and B, have them mark in the same way the finished paragraph from Section 1.7, "Exercise for Busy People." (2) Because Activity D is more difficult, with some classes you may want to save it for review homework in two or three weeks.

1.10   AN INTRODUCTION TO THE NEWSPAPER   (p. 17)

Overview   These activities are intended to familiarize students with newspapers in general and get them ready to begin the Class Newspaper Project. Read Appendix 1 to get an overview of the project and see a sample newspaper. Even if you decide against having your class make a newspaper

(but we hope you won't), you will still find Activities A, B, and C worthwhile for your class.

Before class   Collect copies of fairly recent newspapers in English. You will need one newspaper for every two or three students. You can ask students to buy a specific issue of a particular newspaper so that everyone works with the same material. Or, because Activities A, B, and C can be handled very well with assorted issues of various newspapers, you can ask students and colleagues to help you collect a variety of newspapers over a period of several days.

Activity A: Talking about newspapers
Bring one or more recent newspapers to class. With students' books closed, ask the questions in an informal, conversational fashion. Find out as much as possible about each student's newspaper-reading habits. When you ask about favorite newspaper sections, try to incorporate into the discussion some of the newspaper terminology from Activity B, such as advice column, comic strip, classified ads, horoscopes, and so on. Whenever a specific part of the newspaper is mentioned, find (or have students find) it in the newspapers you brought to class.

Activity B: Getting acquainted with newspapers
Give each pair or small group of students only one newspaper, so students will be forced to work together. Tell students they must discuss each question, agree on an answer, and write it in their books. Since, by design, students will be encountering quite a lot of new vocabulary, expect and welcome the numerous questions that will be posed. Circulate among the students to be readily available for conversation with individuals. Encourage peer help as often as possible by referring a student who does not yet have a given answer to a student who already does. When everyone has finished, bring the class together to discuss the questions and check the answers orally. If a variety of newspapers was used, answers will vary, of course, and you will be able to encourage discussion of specific differences between the newspapers. In this case, students can use the page number in their answers to find the items and show them to the class.

Activity C: Making a classroom display about newspapers
Pair students or form small groups, and give each team one newspaper and a piece of big paper. The teams can share tape and colored markers. Choose items about events currently in the news to complete 13, 14, and 15 in the list – for example, headline about a specific incident in a foreign country, article about a particular development in science, advertisement for a certain new movie – by examining the contents of

the specific newspaper(s) students will be using. If all students have copies of the same issue, dictate items 13, 14, and 15 in the list before students begin their group work. If students have different newspapers, clip a note to each paper with "individualized" items 13, 14, and 15. Have the teams put their displays on the wall when they finish.

Activity D: Beginning a class newspaper
To speed things up in choosing a name of the class newspaper, cut scrap paper into small pieces to use for ideas and balloting. As you list suggested names on the board, reformulate them to sound good in English. Do *not* list anything you will not be happy with later. Remember that the class newspaper will be shown off in many places.

Activity E: Making a masthead for the class newspaper
Students really enjoy this activity, and it will help you identify students who are good printers and designers. Although students will work independently on their own masthead, there will, of necessity, be a lot of collaboration and talking (in English, we hope). Figure 7 is an example of what each student should produce. Collect and save their finished work until the class is ready to lay out an issue of their newspaper. (See Appendix 1 for an explanation of the lay-out procedure.) If you produce more than one issue of the class newspaper, you can spread the glory around by using a different masthead design each time. Even if you need only one masthead, save everything as a source of graphic ideas to use throughout the paper.

Figure 7

1.11   *THE STORY OF A CRIME:*   *Composition/newspaper activity*   (p. 19)

Overview   Because this is the first free composition in the book, we have set out a detailed lesson plan for handling it. This plan describes a process-centered approach to writing for you and your students to follow in this and subsequent sections labeled "composition." In some way, however simple, each "composition" should require students to do more than write a single draft. It should involve them in revising and sharing their work as well.

Plan to devote about thirty minutes in each of five or six sessions to this original paragraph. Don't skimp on time or omit any steps because thoroughness here will lay a strong foundation for future compositions and ultimately save time. Use the remainder of these sessions and homework time for as many structured activities in Unit 2 as possible, including those concerned with editing symbols. Before you begin the first session, go over the following six-day sequence and decide which of the editing methods described in Day 5 you want to use. If you choose the cassette method, ask students on Day 1 to bring cassettes so that you will have them by Day 4.

Although some teachers are initially reluctant to deal with the topic of crime, feeling it is too negative and may stir up painful memories or emotions, you can be assured that the topic has worked well with all types of adult learners. You can read some typical stories in the sample newspaper in Appendix 1.

Day 1: Telling and writing the story of a crime   (1) Begin the assignment by saying to your students, "Get a pencil and paper. I want you to write about a crime. I'm going to write, too. Ready to write? Let's begin." Then, pay undivided attention to your own work, allowing them to sit in silence – perhaps a stunned, puzzled silence – for a few moments.

(2) Break the silence by saying, "Not ready? Want to talk first? Have you ever seen or heard about a crime? What about someone in your family? or a friend? Will you tell us a little about it? What words do you need?" Write new crime vocabulary on the board as you go along. To generate discussion, tell a personal anecdote or part of one as an example. Allow volunteers to tell their experiences, and/or pair students so they can exchange stories. Then ask students to estimate the amount of time they will need to write, but limit the total writing time to 15 to 20 minutes.

(3) In a reassuring manner, explain the four "don'ts" in Activity B, and have students begin writing. As they write, write your story on regular paper (or a ditto mat for easy duplication) with restarts, mark-outs, inserts, no title, and skimpy detail. It is very important that you write a story so you will be able to model each of the upcoming steps. (You could write and make copies of your story ahead of time, but you should still make a pretense of writing it in class.) After about two-thirds of the estimated time has passed, interrupt to check progress, saying "Are you finished? Is your story complete? perfect? Not yet? Well, don't worry. Read this part of your story to a partner. Does your partner understand? Let's try to finish our stories. Don't worry if it is not perfect. Just try to finish." Everyone, including the teacher, continues writing during the remaining minutes.

(4) Stop the work by saying, "Are your stories finished? perfect? No? That's okay. I want to read them. No red pencil...I'll just look. We'll work on them again in the next class." Collect their papers, and pass out copies of your story, saying "Here's my story. I want you to read it. It's not perfect. I want your help." For homework, have students read your story to see if it is finished. Tell them to write three questions to ask you to get more information about the story.

(5) Debrief the students about their feelings. Ask if writing the story was easy or hard and why. Ask what kinds of problems they have writing in English. Listen carefully because their answers will provide valuable insight into their needs and concerns as beginning-level writers.

Day 2: Working with the first draft (adding details)   (1) Have students ask their questions about your story. Write your answers in word, phrase, or sentence form in large handwriting on big paper that can be saved and displayed again later on.

(2) Suggest several adjectives and ask students where to fit them into the story. Time permitting, ask students to suggest other adjectives to insert.

(3) Return the students' stories. To each story, attach a small piece of paper with three or four personalized questions designed to elicit more details from the student about the story. Some of the questions/directions might require students to reorder information, add adjectives, or think about verb tenses, but most will simply seek more content. Have students write answers to the

questions in class, and then collect the stories, questions, and answers.

Day 3: More work with first drafts (topic sentence and title)

(1) Talk about the main idea, or "big meaning," of your paragraph by asking and answering these questions about your story: Why is it important to me? Why did I remember it? How did it change me? How do I feel now because of this? Then return the students' papers, and ask them to think about their own stories and write sentence answers to the same "big meaning" questions. As they write, write your answers on another piece of big paper for later display.

(2) Talk about titles. On a third big sheet of paper, write three possible titles for your story and ask students for opinions about which one is best and why. Then have students write three possible titles for their stories, and put a checkmark beside the best one. Collect the students' papers, big-meaning sentences, and lists of titles.

Day 4: Putting the pieces together and writing a second draft

(1) Model the integration process using your own work. Display the three big pieces of paper: additional content information, big-meaning sentences, and possible titles. Using the board or an overhead transparency, have students watch as you combine the new pieces with your first draft to make a second draft. Talk about what you are doing, and perhaps solicit opinions as you write.

(2) Return students' first drafts and other pieces. Have students work in class to integrate their pieces into a second draft. Then collect the second drafts.

Day 5: Editing and writing the final paper

On this day you and the students will write your final papers in class. You, however, will probably have to finish yours at home since much of your class time will undoubtedly be spent circulating among students to help them with their editing. Prepare for this activity by editing your students' stories in either of two ways. Use the method that is compatible with your resources, but be aware that the cassette method is greatly preferable at this point in the course and more enjoyable to students.

(1) The cassette-editing method requires no more teacher time than traditional marking and does not add any in-class activities to the sequence. It does, however, add an extra homework assignment between Days 4 and 5. For this method, use inexpensive cassette tapes that your students have previously brought in. (Any cassette tape will do, but 30-minute tapes withstand repeated rewinding better than longer ones, and you may want to use them again with later compositions.) On each individual's tape, record the second draft of the student's story. To do this, simply read it onto the tape in good English, correcting grammar mistakes and organizational problems as you go. Use a slow but native speed. Don't break the work into phrase units because students can stop, rewind, and listen as many times as necessry. Return the cassettes but not the second-draft papers. For homework, have students transcribe the recorded version of their stories just as they would a dictation. Have them use either personal cassette players or school machines set up in a language lab or empty classroom. When you collect the transcriptions, mark their errors with the editing symbols in Units 1 and 2. Then, on Day 5, return the marked transcriptions and their unmarked originals, and have students make corrections and write their final papers in class.

(2) If the cassette method is impossible to implement, simply mark the errors in their second drafts with the editing symbols in Units 1 and 2. (See Appendix 2 for a complete list of editing symbols.) Be selective about how many errors you mark so that students will not be overwhelmed and discouraged when you return the papers. Don't be overly concerned about editing for perfect English. Focus on errors affecting comprehension, particularly spelling and verb-tense mistakes, omission of words such as subjects and verbs, and confusing word order. You can edit these papers again, if necessary, if you type them for sharing as described on Day 6.

Day 6: Sharing students' final papers

Here are four methods for sharing the students' final papers.

1. Tape up the stories around the room gallery style. Hand out a list of content questions (at least one per story), and ask students to walk around the room reading the stories and answering the questions.
2. Publish the stories in the class newspaper. Have students read them and answer teacher-produced questions on their content.
3. Type the stories on standard-sized paper, single-spaced to save paper, and make copies for everyone. Have students read, discuss, and ask and answer content questions.
4. Choose two or three of the best stories for

listening-cloze or reading-cloze work. Type or rewrite the stories in a cloze-exercise format by substituting a blank line for every 6th or 7th word. Make copies of the cloze exercises for the students, who must fill the blanks with logical words (reading cloze) or fill them with the words they hear as the story is read aloud (listening cloze). You can read the story "live" or prepare a cassette recording for whole-class or small-group listening.

The handwriting method, listed first, offers the advantage of giving the students an extra incentive to produce neat, legible papers. The typed-version methods, on the other hand, give you the chance to "fix" anything in the papers that might still be incomprehensible to student readers. Typing the papers is particularly advantageous with low-proficiency classes whose papers are short and especially garbled, and in situations when you have not had enough time to treat revision and editing as thoroughly as described here.

1.12   AN INTRODUCTION TO THE COMPOSING PROCESS   (p. 20)

Overview   Once students have finished writing, revising, editing, and sharing their crime-story compositions, they are ready to talk about what they have done and learn some vocabulary to describe the experience. Although composing is an elusive and convoluted process, these drawings make composing seem simple and concrete, and talking about them is a first step toward understanding the process. As the course progresses and students grow in oral proficiency and composing experience, you can return to the drawings and discuss them further.

In class   (1) Discuss the two drawings in Activity A. Help students relate them to recent assignments. Box A illustrates how your students are probably handling structured writing activities assigned as homework and/or how immature writers produce compositions. Box B, on the other hand, shows a more experienced writer working on a composition.

(2) To relate Box B to the students' own experience in writing their crime-story compositions, use the diagram in Figure 8 to

illustrate the steps. Tape the drafts of your story and the big pieces of paper containing your added information to the blackboard in the positions shown in the diagram, and add the arrows and labels with chalk. Review each piece with students. Then ask students to tell you what differences between your first draft and your final paper they can see from their seats. Try to elicit answers such as greater length, typing, title, and so on. Key vocabulary in this discussion are the terms "first draft," "second draft," and "final paper."

(3) Have students look at Activity B. Help them identify and label Paper A as the first draft, B as the second draft, and C as the final paper. Then talk about the five frames in the drawing. Help students identify and label each frame with key vocabulary. Frame 1 is "collecting information," 2 is "writing the first draft," 3 is "revising," 4 is "editing," and 5 is "sharing."

(4) Finally, share your final paper with students in a way that will help them think about how it differs from your first draft. Hand out the typed version of your final paper with blanks for

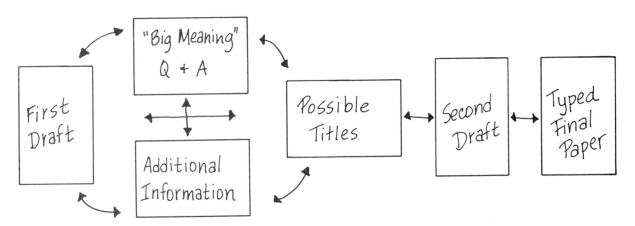

Figure 8

listening-cloze work. Have students listen to a recording of your final paper and fill in the blanks. (Listening in small groups works well if extra equipment is available or if you assign different activities to different groups.) Check the answers orally. For homework, ask students to list 20 words in your final paper that were not in your first draft, a copy of which should be filed in their notebooks.

Unit 2   Getting Acquainted

2.1   *MEET MY CLASS   Composition/newspaper activity*   (p. 22)

Overview   In this section, students compile simple statistics about themselves and use them in a semi-controlled composition. Both homogeneous and heterogeneous groups of students benefit equally from collecting and using the data. Try to do some of the Active Vocabulary Practice on page 27 ahead of time to prepare students for figuring averages.

Activity A: Learning about averages, minimums, maximums, and ranges   Before class, copy (or have a student copy) the table in Activity A on the board. Any version of the drawings will do. Introduce "width," "height," and "depth" by measuring two or three of the students' book bags with a tape measure or ruler. Then read the sentences in Figure 1, which contain information missing from the table. Have a volunteer add the information to the table on the board while the other students write in their books. Finally, have students practice making oral sentences using the model sentence in Activity A before guiding them through the remainder of the activity.

Activity B: Working with paragraph organization   Students may propose and defend more than one sequence of sentences. If, however, they are struggling for even one idea, you can write the headings "home countries" and "new home" on the board and have students put the sentences into one category or the other. Then you can suggest arranging the "home countries" sentences from general/big to specific/little.

Activity C: Using a chart to collect information   Before class, check the chart instructions to see if any of the headings need to be adapted to your particular situation. For example, "Length of time here," which is a cue for "How long have you been here?", could be the length of time in the city, school, program, or class rather than the country. Or, you might change it to "Length of English study" to elicit the question "How long have you studied English?" Although you can usually think of more than one way to frame a question for a given heading, here is one set of possibilities: How old are you? How long have you been in this school? Do you live with your family? Are you married? What is your native language? What did you do in your country? What

---

1. <u>Linda</u> carries a backpack. The person who carries a backpack is <u>Linda</u>.
2. Tom carries a <u>duffle bag</u>. He puts his books and papers in a <u>duffle bag</u>.
3. <u>Kathy</u> carries a tote bag. The person who carries a tote bag is <u>Kathy</u>.
4. John carries a <u>briefcase</u>. He puts his books and papers in a <u>briefcase</u>.
5. The briefcase cost <u>$55</u>. The price of the briefcase was <u>$55</u>.
6. The duffle bag weighs <u>1.5 pounds</u>. The weight of the duffle bag is <u>1.5 pounds</u>.
7. The height of the backpack is <u>17 inches</u>. The backpack is <u>17 inches</u> high.
8. The width of the tote bag is <u>15 inches</u>. The tote bag is <u>15 inches</u> wide.
9. The depth of the briefcase is <u>3½ inches</u>. The briefcase is <u>3½ inches</u> deep.
10. The backpack weighs <u>1 pound</u>. The weight of the backpack is <u>1 pound</u>.

Figure 1

city are you from? How big is it? What continent are you from?

In class, have students close their books and follow the instructions as you read and, whenever necessary, démonstrate them. Or, tell students to read and follow the instructions with a partner or small group.

Activity D: Compiling data   Ordinarily, you would use the summary sheet to compile statistics about the whole class. If, however, your class has more than 20 students, you could have each group (or every two groups) of students who worked together in Activity C fill out their own summary sheet and use their own statistics to write the composition.

Activity E: Writing a newspaper article about your class   This composition is semi-

controlled in that everyone deals with the same content. You can increase control of structure, if necessary, by directing the class's attention to the sentences in Activity B. After students have written up their statistics in composition format, ask "What does this information mean? What general idea does it give about the class?" to elicit concluding/ending sentences about the class. Then elicit several titles orally or in writing. List them on the board, and have students choose their titles from the list.

To follow up, have a fast finisher copy his or her *edited and corrected* composition on a ditto mat as a reading-cloze exercise. Duplicate the cloze and use it for homework or buffer work. Or, use it for in-class listening-cloze work as described on pp. 130–1 (in discussion of Day 6).

2.2   *REVISING:*   "Meet My Class"   (p. 26)

The purpose of this activity is to help students recognize the importance of sequencing information within a paragraph. The overall organization in Box A is better because the information is arranged from general to specific and related sentences are grouped together. Yet, students may see some ways

in which Box B is arguably better than Box A.

This activity and similar "Revising" activities in succeeding units are intended more to stimulate thinking and discussion than to convey a specific answer.

2.3   *ACTIVE VOCABULARY PRACTICE:*   *Mathematics*   (p. 27)

Use Activities A and B in the student pages to introduce the vocabulary associated with arithmetic notations in English. Then during the next few

classes provide additional practice with this vocabulary using Exercises 1 through 4 below.

Exercise 1 (pronunciation of numbers)

Write the information in Figure 2 on the board before giving the commands.

a) 1.5	d) 98.6	g) 11½	j) ⁵⁄₄
b) 1.57	e) ½	h) ¼	k) 12¾
c) 1.572	f) 1½	i) ¾	l) ⅔

Figure 2

Stand up. Stretch.
Touch your toes.
I'm going to read a number.
   Say the *letter* that you see beside that number.

Read the number that I point to.
I'm going to say a letter.
   Read the number beside that letter.
Shake hands.
Sit down.

Exercise 2 (types of problems)

Stand up. Stretch.
Touch your toes.
Lean to the right (left).
I'm going to read a math problem.
 Hold up one finger if the problem
 is addition. Hold up two fingers if
 the problem is subtraction.

Hold up three fingers if the problem is
multiplication. Hold up four fingers if the
problem is division. Ready? (*Read the
problems in Fig. 3.*)
Put both hands on your knees.
Touch your nose with your thumb.
Sit down.

a) $13 + 5 =$ f) $70 \times 1 =$
b) $9 - 4 =$ g) $211 - 0 + 1 =$
c) $3 \times 2 =$ h) $1,000 \div 100 =$
d) $10 \div 5 =$ i) $2,648 - 2,648 =$
e) $1.5 + .5 =$ j) $2\frac{3}{4} + \frac{1}{4} =$

Figure 3

Exercise 3 (dictation of problems)

Send two to five volunteers to the board. Have the other students write at their desks.
Dictate each problem in Figure 3. After students have written down the problems, give
them a couple of minutes to figure the answers. Then have students read each problem
with its answer and tell what kind of problem it is; for example: "Two plus two equals
four. This is an addition problem."

Exercise 4 (harder dictation of problems)

This is a harder form of Exercise 3 for capable, interested students. Dictate problems
like these.

Add 2 and 2.   Divide 6 into 36.
Subtract 7 from 14.   Subtract 10 from 73.
Multiply 25 by 10.   Multiply 100 by 100.
Divide 25 by 5.   Divide 8 into 56.
Add 35 and 0.   Divide 42 by 7.

2.4 THE FAMOUS KENNEDYS: Dictation (p. 28)

This dictation and accompanying activities offer
students a taste of U.S. history and geography. In
general, follow the dictation procedure outlined in
the Teachers' Notes on pages 125–7.

Dictation quiz

Form B The famous Kennedy brothers, John and
Robert, grew up in New England. Their family was
powerful and wealthy. Both were still young when
they entered national politics. Both John and
Robert were assassinated, but they are still famous
today. (39 words)

2.5 SIMILAR SIBLINGS: *Practice text* (p. 30)

In class With students' books closed, have students number from 1 to 5 on scrap paper. Draw two simple faces on the board, label them "Bill" and "Tom," and tell the class to listen carefully to a paragraph about them. Read the paragraph in Figure 4 two or three times. Then read the true-false statements in Figure 4, and have students react to them by writing "true" or "false." Then begin Activity A orally.

Follow-up After completing the sentence combining, make sure students file the papers securely in their notebooks. They will need them in Activity B, whenever you choose to assign it, and later in Unit 5, Section 5.5.

(*Note:* This is one version of the paragraph. There are other possibilities depending on which sentence patterns with the word "both" are used.)

Bill and Tom are native Californians. Both men were born in San Francisco on October 31, 1958. Both have curly black hair and dark brown eyes. Both men are outgoing and love to tell jokes to their friends. Both Bill and Tom have good builds and are very athletic. Both enjoy all kinds of sports. Bill plays football every weekend, and Tom plays on a soccer team. At the university, both men majored in engineering and made good grades. Both graduated in 1980 with B.S. degrees. How can two people have so much in common? Of course, they are identical twins.

True-false statements

1. Bill is from Illinois, and Tom is from California.
2. Bill and Tom are shy.
3. Both like sports.
4. They were not good students.
5. Bill and Tom are brothers.

Figure 4

2.6 WRITING ABOUT YOUR FAMILY: *Composition* (p. 31)

Overview These activities yield a piece of writing that you should help students revise and edit into a composition. They also serve as an introduction to the Family History Project that is begun in this unit and continued in each subsequent unit. Stimulate students' sense of purpose by pointing out that families are a typical topic when people are getting acquainted.

In class The riddles in Activity A can be answered in this way. Riddle 1: The second doctor is a woman and is the boy's mother. Riddle 2: At the table are a woman, her daughter, and her daughter's daughter.

Because students have asked you about your family in Activity C, introduce Activity E by telling them it is your turn to learn something about their families. Handle Activity E as a fluency writing exercise where quantity of writing is very important. Encourage students to leave blanks or substitute words from their own languages if necessary, so as not to interrupt the flow of their writing with vocabulary problems. Then lead students through one or more revision tasks, such as reordering sentences. "Revising: Meet My Family," Section 2.7, is good preparation for this activity. Choose editing and sharing activities, as well as other revision tasks, from the suggestions on pages 130–1.

2.7   REVISING: "Meet my family"   (p. 33)

This activity focuses students' attention on the sequencing of paragraph content as did the previous revising activity in Section 2.2. The overall organization in Box B is better, but students' discussion and defense of aspects of Box A should be encouraged.

2.9   FAMILIES AND FRIENDS AT THE BEACH: Picture composition   (p. 37)

In class   If your students need a little inspiration with the story-planning chart in Activity B, here are a few ideas: WHO: strangers, a baseball team, ex-spouses, our English class; WHY: vacation, someone's birthday, to get out of the house, to meet new people; WHEN: every weekend, two or three times each summer, last year on a holiday, the first day of the summer season.

Sharing   Share the students' stories in one of the ways described on pages 130–1 in Teachers' Notes to Unit 1. Or, share them in a listening-comprehension activity. Read selected pieces to the class, and edit them as you read. Either dictate a straightforward question on the content of each piece before reading it, or read a true-false statement or multiple-choice question afterward.

2.10   A DAY WITH DAD: Practice text   (p. 39)

The basic story is rather long, but students should be able to handle the length because so much of the vocabulary is used in Section 2.9, "Families and Friends at the Beach." Use the three activities in three separate class sessions to avoid boredom. You want to produce facility with the material rather than burnout.

2.11   BEGINNING THE FAMILY HISTORY PROJECT: Composition   (p. 40)

Overview   The Family History Project is a long-range composition project that takes students, step by step over a period of several weeks, through the process of writing an important and "lengthy" piece of family history – a biography of one of their ancestors. This unit contains only the first part of the project. Other parts are presented in each of the succeeding units. In this unit, students decide which family member they will focus on and begin collecting and recording facts, feelings, and recollections about this person to use in their writing. In each of Units 3, 4, 5, and 6, students write a short composition about a specific aspect of their family member. In Unit 6 students also write a simple chronological account of their family member's life. Then they integrate their four short compositions with the chronological account to produce their final paper. Although the process of writing this biography may seem long, it is definitely worth the time and effort. The students' final papers, which may be several pages long, are usually surprisingly good and the source of great pride for both teacher and student.

Before class   Look at *all* the Family History Project activities in the book. They are found on the final pages of Units 2, 3, 4, 5, and 6. Then read the activities in this unit carefully, and decide which family member *you* will write about. As indicated in Activity A, we strongly recommend that you *and* your students choose a family member whom you knew personally, however briefly, and who has already died. We make this recommendation because the biography of a deceased person can be written almost exclusively in the past tense whereas the biography of a living person requires a mixture of present, past, and present-perfect tense verbs. This mixture of tenses is too sophisticated for many students at this level to handle. If you decide, for whatever reason, to give your students the choice of writing about living or deceased family members, be aware of this complication and prepared to give additional assistance when necessary.

   After you have decided on one of your family members, consider your reasons for choosing this person, and prepare to share with students anecdotes, reminiscences, and a brief description of this person in order to spur their thinking and choice. Plan the class session to allow substantial time for discussion (15–20 minutes) and for writing (15–25 minutes).

In class   Share, and encourage students to share, as many family history details as possible while the class works through the introduction in Activity A. Pin down each student's choice early in the discussion. After students write answers to the questions at the end of the introduction, have them transfer their answers to the paper they use to write their "first thoughts" in Activity B.

Quantity is the goal of the "first thoughts" paper, so students need ample time to write, ponder, and write some more. After students use

these papers to fill out the fact sheet in Activity C, collect, read, and *save* them to use again when students write their final paper in Unit 6.

Students need to complete all the items on the Activity C fact sheet before reaching the Family History Project activities in Unit 6. While some students may do this quickly and independently, most will need some assistance from others and regular reminders from you over several weeks to finish it. To get certain facts, students may need to seek help from parents, siblings, or other relatives whenever they telephone, write, or see them in the following weeks. A happy consequence of this consultation process is that many of the families will become interested in the project and become "future readers" of the final papers.

Unit 3   Getting into a Routine

3.1   DR. COOK'S DAILY ROUTINE: *Picture composition*   (p. 43)

Before class   (1) Make your own set of the fifteen picture cues in Activity A to use as a prompt for closed-book oral practice. On standard-sized paper, draw (or ask a student to draw) a simplified version of each frame with colored markers. Make sure each frame is numbered for easy reference. If you are careful when putting up and taking down the frames, they can be used repeatedly. (2) Make a script for Activity A by transferring the words in Figure 1 to the blanks in Activity B. (3) Make an answer key for Activity A by writing the numbers 1 through 15 in random order in the 15 blanks below the pictures.

In class   With students' books closed, display your copies of the fifteen picture cues, and explain the situation described in Activity A. Using your Activity B script, read aloud the series of wake-up

actions. After one or two repetitions, ask students to try to recall the actions in each frame. Then, frame by frame, teach the series of sentences, allowing for both individual and group repetition. When students are comfortable with the vocabulary, have them open their books. Give them the Activity A listening quiz by reading the sentences from your Activity B script in the random order indicated in your answer key.

Activity B   First, have students work independently to fill in the blanks. Tell them to write only one word in each blank. After 2 or 3 minutes, pair the students so they may compare answers. If necessary, interrupt the individual or pair work to reread all the sentences to the students one or more times. Check by writing (or having students write) the completed sentences on the

1. gets, at	6. washes, her	11. dries, hair
2. gets, of	7. rinses, hair	12. brushes, teeth
3. goes, the	8. gets, of, bathtub	13. puts, her
4. gets, the, bathtub	9. dries, with	14. puts, on, clothes
5. takes, shower	10. combs, her	15. goes, the, kitchen, breakfast

Figure 1

board. For homework, tell students to memorize the sentences in Activity B by rewriting them several times. At the following class meeting, test their memorization by displaying in random order some (or all) of your picture cues and asking students to write the corresponding sentences on a piece of paper. Collect and check their work.

Activity C   Use your display set of picture cues to demonstrate and practice combining sentences with "before" and "after." Have students continue practicing with a partner.

Activities D and E   These activities provide students with written practice in forming and punctuating complex sentences with "before" and "after." Have students do part of each activity orally and without taking notes before beginning to write. Activities D.3 and E may be assigned as written homework.

Follow-up   Several days after completing the other activities, use Activity F for additional oral and written practice.

3.2 JIM STAMP'S DAY: Practice text (p. 46)

Before class   Prepare an answer key by transferring the words in Figure 2 to the blanks in Activity A on pages 46–7 of your book. In some instances, you and the students may agree to substitute alternate words.

In class   Begin by having the whole class skim the text in Activity A to answer these questions:
1) How many paragraphs are there? 2) What is the general topic of each paragraph? 3) Which paragraph is the longest? 4) How many lines are in the introduction? Continue by reading aloud the introduction to clarify the situation and any vocabulary questions students may have. Then pair or group students and ask them to try to fill in the blanks in Paragraph 1. After checking, have students put down their pencils, listen, and read along silently as you read Paragraph 2. Then ask

them to fill in the blanks in Paragraph 2 with the words they heard. Check as a class, and then do Paragraphs 3 and 4 in the same manner. Continue with Activity B or assign it as homework.

Activity C is designed to build fluency through intensive in-class oral practice. Whether you handle it in a straightforward manner or develop it as a "quiz-show" team competition, keep students' attention focused on learning the content, that is, all the details about Jim Stamp's day. Activity D may be done immediately afterward, but it is better to wait until a later class session. Use Activity D as a fluency-building exercise and as a test of the students' ability to recall information. Encourage students to concentrate on writing down as many factual details as possible without worrying about making mistakes.

Paragraph 1: up, get, shower, shave, on, shoes, kitchen, eating, the, son, leave, takes, takes, hospital, Then

Paragraph 2: begins, of, Next, am, nurses, walk, check, for, a, finally, Sometimes, take, busy, paperwork, ends, leave

Paragraph 3: the, Before, takes, so, way, as, quickly, feel, breakfast, repair, shopping, tired, to, come, Unfortunately, I'm, of, soon, must

Paragraph 4: to, newest, don't, tired, miss, I'm, rarely, hope, can, day

Figure 2

3.3 A ROUTINE DAY: Composition (p. 50)

Overview   This is the first, and the most structured, of the three compositions students will write in this unit. Allow at least 50 minutes for

students to do the Activity A interviews, write the Activity B first drafts, and read their partners' papers. When students read their partner's paper, have them look for and tell their partner about any factual mistakes and/or confusing sentences. Although you will need to collect and read the first drafts to choose appropriate revising and editing tasks, here are some suggestions.

Revision tasks 1) Adding details. Assuming students have corrected all factual errors to their partners' satisfaction, have students find the sentence(s) in their papers that answer(s) question 2 in Activity A. Next, ask them to count the number of "before-school" actions they described in the sentence(s). If their papers tell about only one or two actions, have them write, at the bottom of the paper or on a clean sheet, a new sentence telling about at least two more actions. Obviously, they may need to consult their partner for additional information. Repeat this procedure with questions 6, 11, and 13. In the second draft, have students incorporate their four new sentences in logical places.

2) Paragraphing. Draw the editing symbol "¶" on the board, and discuss how it is used to show changes in paragraph organization. Have students count the number of paragraphs in their compositions, and explain the general topic of each. If appropriate, talk about at least two good ways to paragraph the information in this composition. Have students use the new "¶" editing symbol to mark any changes they need to make in the paragraph organization of their compositions.

Editing tasks Before you mark their compositions in any way, have students try to find and correct some or all of these common problems. It is best for the class to deal separately with each type

of problem before beginning with another type.
- Are all the verbs in the simple present tense?
- Are the pronouns (he/him/his or she/her/her) used correctly?
- Does each sentence begin with a capital letter and end with a period?
- Is the person's name used in the first sentence of each paragraph?

After your class has done all or most of the activities in "Editing: Fragments" (p. 54), ask students to find and correct this type of editing problem in their compositions. Use these or similar questions to prompt their work.
- How many sentences have words like "before," "after," "when," etc.? If your answer is 1 or 0, use these words to combine at least two pairs of short sentences.
- Do all the sentences (new and old) with words such as "before," "after," and "when" have a subject and a verb in both the main clause and the subordinate clause?

To do these editing tasks, students should work with a partner. First, they should read their own papers with an eye toward correcting a specific type of problem. Then they should exchange papers and look for the same type of problem in their partners' paper. However, rather than trying to correct their partners' errors, students should merely circle errors they find and explain to the author, if necessary, why something is wrong. During this editing process, make yourself available at your desk, or circulate around the classroom to answer questions and settle disputes. Either in class or for homework, have students rewrite their compositions with all necessary revising and editing changes before giving it to you for final editing.

3.4 VICTOR COOK'S BREAKFAST: *Practice text* (p. 51)

Before class Prepare "flashcards" to prompt oral practice of Wh-questions based on the text. With colored markers, write each of the words or phrases in Figure 3 on a separate piece of standard-sized scrap paper.

bread	the news on T.V.
breakfast	the weather report
eggs	on the radio
coffee, milk, and	his girlfriend, Ellen
juice	in another city

Figure 3

In class (1) With students' books closed, read the text aloud once or twice. Then have students write "true" or "false" on a piece of scrap paper in response to these oral statements:

1. Victor has breakfast every morning.
2. Victor and Ellen are neighbors.
3. Victor eats breakfast at work.
4. Victor is going to have eggs, toast, juice, milk, and tea.
5. Victor's mind isn't on the weather report.

Ask students to open their books to the text, call on volunteers to read it aloud, and check answers to the true-false exercise.

≫→

(2) Practice oral question formation with the 8 flashcards from Figure 3. Tell students that each flashcard gives the answer to a Wh-question. As you show each flashcard, call on individual students to ask the corresponding question. Practice until your students can perform fluently.

(3) Have students do the first part of Activity A orally and without taking notes before assigning it as written homework. Activity B can be assigned at a later date as written homework for the whole class or used as in-class buffer work for fast finishers.

3.5   ACTIVE VOCABULARY PRACTICE: *Shapes and symbols*   (p. 52)

Although the vocabulary of shapes and symbols is generally useful, students will need it specifically for "Special Exercise 6: Secret diagrams" in Unit 4. (See p. 149 for instructions.) First, practice in class with shapes and symbols, using Exercises 1, 2, and 3 below in several class sessions. Then assign the written matching exercise in the student pages (p. 52) as follow-up homework. As a part of checking the matching exercise, ask students to identify which items are:
– marks of punctuation
– symbols used with numbers

– symbols (shapes) used in geometry
– symbols usually found on a typewriter
Exercise 4 (late breakfast) reinforces daily routine vocabulary, especially that in Section 3.4, "Victor Cook's Breakfast: Practice Text." It can be used effectively before, during, or even after other work in Unit 4, so feel free to use it whenever it seems appropriate.

Exercise 1 (shapes)

As this drill progresses, *draw* the items that you need on the board. Once an item has been practiced, send individual students to draw it too.

Stand up. Stretch.
Put your hands on your hips (waist).
Twist to the right (left).
Put both hands on top of your head.
Put both hands high above your head.
Point to the triangle (circle, rectangle, square) in the center of the board.

Point to the circle in the lower left-hand corner of the board (in the right half of the board).
Point to the biggest rectangle (the smallest square).
Joe, please go to the board and draw a triangle (a small triangle, a small square to the right of the circle, a big triangle in the circle under the "No Smoking" sign, etc.)

Exercise 2 (symbols and shapes)

Point to/Draw:

checkmark	parentheses	diamond
number sign	comma	equal sign
dollar sign	colon	letters of alphabet, both capital and lowercase
percent sign	asterisk	forms (Give extra attention to those letters,
question mark	flower	such as vowels, that your students find
exclamation mark	star	troublesome.)
period	heart	roman numerals

Exercise 3 (shapes)

Find examples of rectangles, squares, circles, and triangles in the classroom. Students are often quite eager and inventive with this activity. Typical examples are blackboard, clock, watches, tabletops, desktops, table bases, ceiling tiles, floor tiles, windows, bulletin board, students' belongings and supplies.

Exercise 4 (late breakfast)

Close your eyes. Sleep.
Take a little nap.
Wake up. Stretch.
Put your napkin in your lap.
Pour a cup of coffee.
Put in two spoons of sugar.
Pour in a little milk.
Stir the coffee five times.
Shake salt and pepper on the scrambled
   eggs.

Pour syrup on your pancakes.
Pick up your knife.
Pick up your fork.
Cut your pancakes.
Look at your watch.
Open your mouth and eyes wide!
Hit your cheek!
Throw your napkin on the table.
Don't eat!
Run to work!

3.6 *EDISON'S TYPICAL WORKING DAY: Dictation* (p. 53)

Overview   This dictation introduces Thomas Edison, who is the subject of a series of activities in Units 5 and 6. Before you begin, familiarize yourself with these activities, which appear in Sections 5.4, 6.2, and 6.3. As you will see, some future Edison activities assume that students have learned and can recall the facts about Edison's life that were presented in prior units. Therefore, it is important that you handle this dictation and related activities thoroughly and enthusiastically. Some classes also need the incentive of one or more "pop quizzes" to begin paying attention to the facts.

In class   In general, follow the dictation

procedure outlined in the Unit 1 Teachers' Notes on pages 125–7. If your students have by this time discovered that Form B always appears in the Teachers' Notes, simply make a few small changes in the text so that memorization will not be helpful.

Dictation quiz

Form B   Thomas Edison had an unusual daily routine. He frequently worked twenty hours out of twenty-four, stopped only for short naps, and made over 1,000 inventions. Despite too much coffee and too many cigars, he lived actively to the age of 84. (41 words)

3.7 *EDITING: Fragments* (p. 54)

Use this group of activities after finishing Section 3.1, "Dr. Cook's Daily Routine," but before reaching the editing stage on the compositions in 3.9, "Letters about a Perfect Routine," and 3.12, "Family History Project." Keep the focus more on

understanding fragment errors than on mastering the grammar terms used in the activities. Students will receive the maximum benefit from Activities B and D if you focus on alternate, correct ways of expressing the same idea.

3.8 EDITING: *Editing symbols* (p. 56)

Do these activities just before students write their final drafts of Section 3.3, "A Routine Day." Activities A and B are best handled in class, whereas Activities C and D are appropriate for written homework assignments.

3.9 LETTERS ABOUT A PERFECT ROUTINE: *Composition/newspaper activity* (p. 60)

Both you and the students will really enjoy doing this, the second of the three compositions in this unit. Be sure to write along with your students. If possible, write yours on a ditto mat and quickly make copies so that you and the students can exchange papers immediately.

For homework ask students to read your paper, then take the role of teacher and write three questions about the text to ask other students to check their reading comprehension. Collect the students' questions, read them to the class (reformulating as you go so that you are reading grammatically correct questions), and elicit answers.

Return the students' papers. Ask students to reread their work, and add one or more final sentences that answer the question, "Why is this the perfect routine for you?" Collect the papers again. If time allows, have students thoroughly revise and edit their work. If not, choose a sharing procedure from among those described on pages 130 and 136. Put one or more of the best papers in the class newspaper under the headline "Psychology Corner."

3.10 REVISING: *"An Imaginary Day"* (p. 61)

In Box B the amount of detail given each part of the day is balanced overall. In Box A detailed attention is given only to activities before school; however, the case might be made that the details in Box A make that draft more interesting and thus better. As you and your class come to your own conclusion, point out to students that in working with their own drafts they may need to combine good elements from one draft with good elements from another.

3.11 CROSSWORD PUZZLES: *Newspaper activity* (p. 62)

Crossword puzzles are easy to make, fun to solve, and provide valuable practice in forming Wh-questions. To prepare students to make their own puzzles, have them practice with Activities A and B. The answers for Activity A are shown in Figure 4. There are many possible questions for each word in Activity B. Any logical and correctly formed Wh-question should be considered correct. When students are ready to make their own puzzles, get them started by demonstrating on the board the steps in Activity C. For homework, ask students to finish their puzzles and make a clean, blank copy in pencil or black ink. Collect both versions.

Figure 4

Follow-up Choose some of the best puzzles, and make enough copies of them to share with the class. Use these puzzles as a change-of-pace classroom activity, as homework, and as buffer work for your fast finishers. If your class is making a newspaper, put one or more in the next issue. (Save space by using a copier to reduce the size of the grid and the cues.)

3.12 FAMILY HISTORY PROJECT – ROUTINE DAY: Composition   (p. 64)

Overview This family history paper, unlike the "first thoughts" paper on page 41 in Unit 2, should be treated as a "major" piece of work, to be written, revised, edited, and rewritten in final polished form. This process will not only take several days to complete, but will also cause students to produce a number of pages of written work. The same will be true for the family history activities in succeeding units. Therefore, you should decide what kind of filing system you and your students will use to collect and organize the drafts of this and other family history papers in the coming weeks. You may want to keep track of each individual's growing collection yourself, whether in a folder or merely in a big clip. Or, you might ask students to create a special section in their notebooks for filing these papers.

How you direct students' revision of the routine day paper should depend, as always, on the organizational and content problems in their first drafts. You are likely to find, however, that students will benefit from revision tasks that require them to:
– add year, age, and place details;
– add time markers, such as "in the evening," "at 9 a.m.," "before . . .";
– add information about parts of the day they initially ignored;
– add details about life in the past, such as in activity A;
– arrange information according to time of day;
– put verbs in the past tense.
To create material for revision practice, draft a paragraph about your own family member's daily routine, either in class while students write theirs or at home after reading their first drafts. Produce a paper that contains some of the same revision problems as your students'. Present your draft in a way that will familiarize students with its content and structure – perhaps as a reading-cloze or listening-cloze exercise with past tense verbs and time markers omitted. Follow up with a true-false quiz covering the content of your draft. Next, choose from the following suggestions those revision tasks best suited to your particular class. Have students do each task, first as a class using *your* draft and then independently using their own first drafts. Complete one task before going on to another.

Revision tasks (1) Have students circle all the time markers in your paragraph, which might be written so as to include many such markers near the beginning and none at the end. Ask students to help you decide where to add additional markers. Then have them mark their own drafts and add two or three more time markers to their own papers as you direct.

(2) Have students list, as in Activity B, the routine activities mentioned in your draft. (Make sure that your draft does not describe certain parts of the day.) Propose additional sentences and have the students assist in deciding on their placement in your paragraph. Then have them analyze their own drafts in a similar fashion and add one or more sentences about one or more parts of the day.

(3) Have students read your draft to find the year and place of your family member's routine, and his or her age at that time. After finding all three in your paragraph, ask them to circle this same information in their own drafts and add any of these facts that might be missing.

(4) Have students find within your draft the ways in which your family member's life was different from the life of today's teenagers. Have them identify and/or add similar details to their papers.

(5) Have students take home your first draft and write three questions to ask you about its content. Write your answers to their questions on the blackboard and enlist their aid in deciding where to add the new information. Return their papers with three questions for them. After they answer the questions, have them revise to add the new information.

Unit 4   Describing Places

4.1   SOUTH AMERICAN NEIGHBORS: Practice text   (p. 66)

In class   (1) The mapwork in Activity A is the key to bringing this text to life. Once you have finished with the mapwork, ask students to close their books. Preview Activity B with the following listening comprehension work.

(2) Matching. Use the material in Figure 1, which contains the combined sentences in Activity B, a vocabulary list, and definitions of some words in the list. Write the vocabulary list on the board. Ask students to number from 1 to 8 on scrap paper. Read the paragraph in Figure 1 two times. Then, read the eight definitions one at a time, and ask students to find and write down the vocabulary item that matches each definition. After you check, elicit definitions for the five vocabulary items that do not match the definitions in Figure 1.

(3) True-false. Ask students to number from 1 to 5 on the same piece of paper. With their books still closed, read the combined paragraph in Figure 1 two more times. Then read these statements and have students respond to them by writing "true" or "false."

1. Brazil is smaller than Bolivia.
2. Bolivia lies north of the equator.
3. Bolivia doesn't have a coastline.
4. Brazil is not an independent nation.
5. The mountains in Bolivia are higher than the ones in Brazil.

Follow-up   Have students make sentences with "both" and "but" to compare and contrast their own countries with a given country. Time permitting, you might ask them to develop their ideas into a short paragraph.

4.2   THE PROUD STATE OF TEXAS: Dictation   (p. 68)

This dictation and accompanying activities give students an opportunity to explore a bit of American history and geography. The general procedure for dictations is outlined in the Teachers' Notes to Unit 1 on page 125. In Part II of Activity B, encourage students to look for answers in a dictionary or an encyclopedia, or ask an outside person familiar with the U.S. In case one of these resources is not available, here are the answers.

6. There are 50 states in the U.S. They are represented by the 50 stars in the flag. / The thirteen original states were Connecticut, Delaware, Georgia, Massachusetts, Maryland, New Hampshire, New Jersey, New York, North Carolina, Pennsylvania, Rhode Island, South Carolina, and Virginia. / Both Hawaii and Alaska became states in 1959, but Hawaii became part of the United States later in the year than Alaska. / Texas became a state in 1845.
7. To approximate the distance, multiply 13 hours by 65 mph (104 kph) = 845 miles (1,352 km). The maximum legal speed for driving in Texas is 65 mph. 1 mile = 1.6 kilometers.
8. New Mexico, Oklahoma, Arkansas, Louisiana, and Mexico. / Spanish.
9. Dallas: assassination of President Kennedy; famous in the 1970–1980s for the TV show *Dallas.* / Houston: largest city and port in Texas; Johnson Space Center (NASA); excellent medical center. / San Antonio: the Alamo and other Spanish missions; large Spanish-speaking population; and annual Fiesta celebration. / Capital: Austin.
10. Oil wells: all over the state / cattle ranches: all over the state, but the biggest ranches are in the southern and western parts of the state. / oranges and grapefruit: in the Rio Grande Valley, the southern tip of the state. / rice fields: along the Gulf coast. / pine forests: in East Texas.

Dictation quiz

Form B   Texas is famous around the world for its cowboys, cattle ranches, oil wells, and size. It takes about thirteen hours to drive across the state. Texans were upset in 1959 when Alaska became the biggest state. They joked that it could melt because it was mainly ice. According to proud Texans, Texas is still the largest state. (57 words)

Combined sentences in Activity B

   Brazil and Bolivia are countries in South America. Brazil is almost as large as the United States, but Bolivia is only one-tenth as big. Both Brazil and Bolivia have good farmlands, rich mines, and dense forests. Brazil has a long coastline, many rivers, and low mountains, but Bolivia has no coastline, few rivers, and many tall mountains. The tallest mountain in Bolivia is more than 21,000 feet high, but the highest mountain in Brazil is under 10,000 feet. Both countries lie south of the equator in the tropics. The climate of Brazil is uniformly warm and humid; however, the climate of Bolivia varies with the altitude. Indians lived in both countries for many years before any Europeans arrived. The Portuguese settled in Brazil in the fifteenth century, but the Spanish didn't come to Bolivia until the sixteenth century. Today both countries are independent nations with many natural resources. Both Brazil and Bolivia are working hard to develop their resources.

Vocabulary

coastline	hills	the tropics
dense forests	river	uniformly
desert	mines	valleys
the equator	natural resources	
fifteenth century	sixteenth century	

Definitions

1. the place where the land touches the ocean
2. the imaginary line around the earth halfway between the South Pole and the North Pole
3. where there are many trees close together
4. a hot, humid area near the equator
5. the same everywhere
6. places under the ground where people dig for gold, silver, coal, and other things
7. things in nature that people can use to make life better, such as water, forests, oil, tin, diamonds, and so on
8. the 1500s, that is, from 1500 to 1599

Figure 1

4.3 MY HOMETOWN: *Composition/newspaper activity* (p. 70)

Overview This composition should be treated as a major piece of work to be revised, edited, and shared with others. The activities in "Editing: Punctuation" (p. 73) and "Editing: Run-ons" (p. 74) will be useful at the editing stage.

In class (1) If your students come from the same hometown, tell them to write for readers who are not familiar with their town. After each student has written a final paper, work together to produce a composite composition. To do this, have the students read (or listen to you read) each other's work to find and list good ideas and sentences to use in the composite. As a group, decide how to organize the information and write the composite composition.

   (2) If your students come from different hometowns, they will enjoy learning about the places their classmates come from. After the students have finished their final papers, choose one or more of these ways for students to share their work.
a) Read the students' papers (or excerpts from them) to the class, and have the listeners guess which town is being described.

》》》→

b) If the class is making a newspaper, use a guessing-game format to publish excerpts. Appendix 1 contains a sample.
c) If you are not making a newspaper, create a handout based on the above suggestions. Or,

have students recopy their final drafts, leaving out the name of their hometowns and their own names. Then post the compositions and have students guess which city each one is describing.

4.7 HOMETOWN WEATHER REPORT: *Newspaper activity* (p. 76)

These activities are fun to do and produce an interesting and attractive graphic for the class newspaper or for periodic classroom display. Students with any interest at all in math or science welcome the "technical," albeit simple, vocabulary

used to devise it. Activities C and D make good change-of-pace homework assignments. For *your* inspiration, see a sample weather report in Appendix 1.

4.8 SURVEY OF FAVORITE CITIES: *Newspaper activity* (p. 77)

Before class Locate informants for your students to interview. Other English-speaking teachers and school administrators are generally sympathetic participants. Your English-speaking friends and acquaintances outside of school may also be willing to receive a phone call from a student interviewer. If there are not enough informants to go round, send students in pairs or even groups of three to talk to one person.

Follow-up (1) Put the survey reports in the newspaper along with the weather report and the "My Hometown" article(s) to make a travel section or issue. (2) Create a reading-comprehension exercise based on the content of the students' reports.

4.9 A TRIP TO TOKYO: *Practice text* (p. 78)

In class With students' books closed, write the first three questions in Figure 2 on the board. Read the text to students, and elicit oral answers to the questions. Then, read the text again, and ask the last three questions in Figure 2. Finally, have students open their books and work *orally* through the first part of the text before assigning Activity A as written homework.

Follow-up (1) Several days or weeks later, use this text to provide oral tense-change practice. Have student 1 change sentence 1 (to the past tense, for example), student 2 change sentences 1 and 2, student 3 change sentences 1, 2, and 3, and so on. Students usually perceive this activity as a

game. By the end, several are usually eager to try the whole thing.

(2) Here are two more changes that can be made on the basic text:
— Pretend you are Tina. You have just returned from a trip to Tokyo. Write a letter to your mother and tell her what you did. Begin your letter this way: "Dear Mother, I spent my vacation...."
— Pretend you are Tina's husband, Ted. Your wife will soon go to Tokyo. Write a letter to your mother and tell her what Tina will do. Begin your letter this way: "Dear Mother, This year Tina will spend...."

1. What is Tina carrying?
2. Name three things that Tina is doing.
3. Is Tina's friend at home?
4. Is the weather sunny?
5. Where is Tina staying?
6. Is Tina's vacation inexpensive?

Figure 2

4.10 ACTIVE VOCABULARY PRACTICE: *Following directions* (p. 79)

Overview   Students really enjoy this section of six exercises which require writing and/or following instructions for "secret diagrams." Only one of the exercises, the fifth in the sequence, is given in the student pages. The opening four exercises and the final exercise appear only here.

The element of secrecy in these six exercises together with the immediacy of concrete feedback creates a pleasant gamelike atmosphere in the classroom. These exercises are designed to provide practice with prepositions and useful words in writing about places, and to review basic vocabulary used in directions in textbooks, tests, applications, and various forms. Most of the vocabulary was introduced in Units 1 and 3. Do only one of these exercises per class session. Monitor students' progress by circulating and checking as they work, by having them compare their papers with a classmate's or a model you provide, and/or by collecting and checking their papers.

Exercise 1: Direction Dictation (Days of the Week)

> Read these instructions, pausing in between so students can act. Demonstrate only when necessary.
>
> 1. Take out a sheet of paper.
> 2. Print your full name, last name first, in the upper right-hand corner.
> 3. Write today's date under your name.
> 4. Print the title "The Days of the Week" in the middle of the top line.
> 5. Number from 1 to 7 along the left margin.
> 6. Write "Sunday" beside #1, "Monday" beside #2, "Tuesday" beside #3, etc.
> 7. Draw a circle to the right of "Sunday."
> 8. Draw a rectangle around "Monday."
> 9. Put a triangle to the left of "Tuesday" in the margin.
> 10. Circle "Wednesday."
> 11. Draw a line through "Thursday."
> 12. Underline "Friday."
> 13. Cross out "Saturday."
> 14. Fold your paper in half.
> 15. Draw a big rectangle on the outside of your paper and sign your name above it.

Exercise 2: Direction Dictation (Assorted)

> Read these instructions, demonstrating only when necessary.
>
> 1. Take out a sheet of paper.
> 2. Number from 1 to 12 beside the left margin line.
> 3. Print "classwork" in the middle of the top line.
> 4. Print your last name only in the upper right-hand corner of the page.
> 5. Write "Monday" beside #2.
> 6. Circle #8.
> 7. Put a checkmark beside #11.
> 8. Underline "Monday."
> 9. Write "January" to the left of #4.
> 10. Cross out "January."
> 11. Draw a triangle in the center of the page.
> 12. Draw a flower above the triangle.
> 13. Draw a car in the lower left-hand corner of the page.
> 14. Write "the end" in the middle of the bottom line.
> 15. Fold your paper in half lengthwise.
> 16. Sign your name on the outside.
> 17. Put the paper under your right elbow.

>>>→

Exercise 3: Direction Dictation (Seasonal – Christmas card)

Use as written at the appropriate time of year. Adapt for other holidays. Read the instructions, demonstrating only as necessary.

1. Take out a piece of paper.
2. Fold it in half lengthwise.
3. Put the paper on your desk with the fold on the left side.
4. Draw a triangle in the center of the page with a point up.
5. On top of this point draw a star.
6. In the middle of the bottom of the triangle, draw a rectangle.
7. Draw five little circles inside the triangle.
8. Write "Merry" above the star.
9. Write "Christmas" below the rectangle.
10. Open the paper.
11. Write "and a Happy New Year!" inside.
12. Sign your name below "and a Happy New Year!"

Exercise 4: Reading "Secret" Directions

Before class, duplicate (or copy by hand) the "secret" directions in Figure 3. Each set fits nicely on one-quarter of a standard-sized page. You will need enough copies of Set I for half of your class, and enough copies of Set II for the other half. To convey a sense of secrecy, fold each set and mark "I" (or "II") boldly on the outside. For ease of distribution, put all folded Set I's in one envelope and all folded Set II's in another. With a little attention you can collect them after doing the activity in class, and use them in class after class.

Set I	Set II
1. Take out a sheet of paper.	1. Take out a sheet of paper.
2. Number from 1 to 7 along the left-hand margin.	2. Number from 1 to 12 along the left margin.
3. Write "February" in the lower left-hand corner.	3. Draw a circle in the lower right-hand corner.
4. Draw a rectangle in the center on the page.	4. Write "English" beside #2.
5. Circle "February."	5. Sign your name above the circle.
6. Print your first name beside #6.	6. Cross out "English."
7. Underline your name.	7. Put an X beside #3.
8. Draw a cat in the upper right-hand corner.	8. Draw a bird in the upper left-hand corner.
9. Fold your paper into thirds.	9. Fold your paper in half lengthwise.

Figure 3

In class, put the words in Figure 4 on the board. Practice their pronunciation with the class. Ask for a definition and/or demonstration of each.
Have students work in pairs. Give Partner A the "secret" directions in Set I. Partner A reads the directions to Partner B but does not let Partner B see them. Partner B listens and acts. When the pair finishes, give Partner B the "secret" directions in Set II, and have the partners reverse roles. Be sure to collect all directions so you can use them again.

Exercise 5: Following Directions

This exercise is section 4.10 in the student pages. Assign it as homework. To check, have students compare papers, or collect the papers to monitor individual proficiency.

checkmark	print
fold in half/fourths/thirds	square
circle (n. & v.)	margin
number (n. & v.)	rectangle
sign (v.)	triangle
draw	

Figure 4

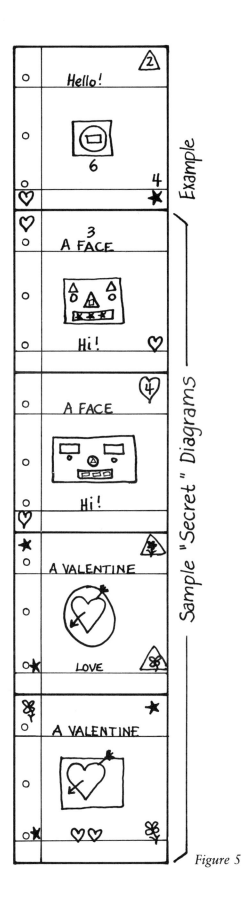

Figure 5

Special Exercise 6: Secret Diagrams

Before class, copy the five diagrams in Figure 5 on notebook paper with bright markers or pens. Make enough additional diagrams so that each pair of students has a somewhat different version to work with. (Again, with a little care, you can use the diagrams numerous times.)

Day 1 (1) Show the example diagram, elicit instructions for reproducing it, and write the instructions on the board. To make these instructions easier to follow, ask students to divide them into Part I, Part II, and Part III. Students usually suggest dividing them according to the top, middle, and bottom of the page. Then hide the diagram, and ask the class to follow the instructions to see if they work. Leave instructions on the board for reference.

(2) Give each pair of students a secret diagram and tell them not to show it to anyone. Give the face diagrams to abler students. Have each pair work together and write one set of instructions for reproducing their diagram. Tell them to write their instructions on one sheet of paper and put both of their names on it. When they finish, have them follow their own instructions to see if they are accurate. Then have each pair clip their instructions to the diagram before turning them in. After class, mark grammar mistakes with editing symbols, but don't change the content or organization of the instructions.

Day 2 Return the instructions but not the diagrams. Have the same partners work together to make corrections. Then ask each person to make and turn in a corrected, final copy.

Day 3 Give each student a paper other than his own or his partner's. Have each student draw a diagram according to the instructions. Then tape up your original diagrams. Ask students to match the originals to their reproductions. If two diagrams are not exactly alike, work with the students to determine whether the problem lies with the writer or the reader.

4.11   CLASS TRIP: *Composition/newspaper activity*   (p. 80)

Overview   A field trip is a terrific teaching tool, but where you go and what you do there are not of the utmost importance. What counts the most is exploiting the shared experience as a stimulus for talking and writing. Activities A and B offer a framework for preview. If you need information about times, prices, etc., have students make the necessary phone calls after role play and encouragement. Even if you already have such information yourself, you may want to pretend otherwise to give your students a valuable experience. If you and your students choose a museum, gallery, or other type of exhibition, you can play the following detective game during the visit.

Detective game   Before the trip, make game forms as shown in Figure 6. At some point during the visit, give each player the three forms. Ask each player to choose a painting (drawing, photo, object, etc.) and fill out the three forms. (If there is an odd number of players, you must play too.) Collect the completed forms, and sort them so that the title pages (Form 1) are together, the location pages (Form 2) are together, and the description pages (Form 3) are together.

Divide the players into two teams. Give each team the description pages (Form 3) from the other team. Tell the teams to read a description, find the matching painting, and write the title and artist on the description page. If a team cannot find a specific painting, hand out the location page as a

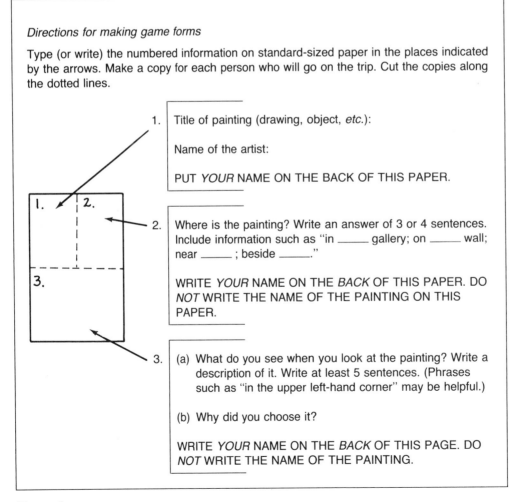

Directions for making game forms

Type (or write) the numbered information on standard-sized paper in the places indicated by the arrows. Make a copy for each person who will go on the trip. Cut the copies along the dotted lines.

1.   Title of painting (drawing, object, *etc.*):

Name of the artist:

PUT *YOUR* NAME ON THE BACK OF THIS PAPER.

2.   Where is the painting? Write an answer of 3 or 4 sentences. Include information such as "in _____ gallery; on _____ wall; near _____ ; beside _____."

WRITE *YOUR* NAME ON THE *BACK* OF THIS PAPER. DO *NOT* WRITE THE NAME OF THE PAINTING ON THIS PAPER.

3.   (a) What do you see when you look at the painting? Write a description of it. Write at least 5 sentences. (Phrases such as "in the upper left-hand corner" may be helpful.)

(b) Why did you choose it?

WRITE *YOUR* NAME ON THE *BACK* OF THIS PAGE. DO *NOT* WRITE THE NAME OF THE PAINTING.

Figure 6

help. When a team has matched all descriptions with paintings, check the answers against the title pages. The team that finishes first is the winner.

Activity C: Written report

(1) This report on the class trip can be published in the class newspaper, as shown in Appendix 1, or sent to a school administrator as an "official record" of the trip. After the trip but before the following class, write questions that will elicit an account of the trip. Include questions that call for description and opinion as well as narration so that students must consider more than chronological order in organizing their reports. Copy your questions on slips of paper, and scramble them in an envelope. If you want students to work in groups, set up an envelope for each group. Here is a sample set of questions to use as a point of departure. They were written after a trip to a museum.

How many people went on the trip?
What was your opinion of the trip?
What did you do at the museum?
Tell about lunch. (Where did you eat? What did you eat?)
What was the museum like? (Describe the museum.)
When did you go home?
How did you go home?

How did you get to the museum?
When did you arrive?
Who met the group at the museum? When? Where?
What did you like best?
What happened after lunch?
When did you meet at school?
When did you leave school?
What happened on June 7?

(2) Have one student at a time draw a question out of the envelope and read it to the other students. When the group has agreed on an answer, have a student "secretary" write it on the board or big paper. If any students were absent on the day of the trip, have them take turns acting as questioners and secretaries. When all the sentences are on the board, go back and edit them with as much student participation as possible. Then have students work independently to organize the sentences into a written report to turn in to you.

(3) When you read the students' reports, focus on the organizational and paragraphing strategies. Choose two or three reports that employ different strategies, and type or copy them for students to read in class. Have students decide which report is best and tell why. Publish the preferred version in the class newspaper. Or, have its author rewrite it in the form of a memorandum and actually deliver it to a school administrator.

4.12   FAMILY HISTORY PROJECT – IMPORTANT PLACE: Composition   (p. 81)

Overview   The starting point for the "important place" composition is the Family History Project folder or notebook section. Some students may find only one place mentioned and have to ponder a bit to build even a small list of places to choose from. Indeed, some students may be writing about family members who lived all their lives in a single place. This place may even be the student's own hometown, already described in "My Hometown" (p. 70). In such cases, students will be tempted to copy directly from their earlier pieces unless you help them widen their focus to a region or narrow it to a farm or neighborhood.

Have students describe the place as it was in one year or time period in the past. Make sure students specify the year(s) in the paragraphs to make it easier for them to integrate the paragraphs into the final papers later on and, of course, to keep them writing in the past tense.

Students who are intimately familiar with the place they are describing may also wish to describe how this place is today in order to show how it has changed. Such a comparison, however, should not be the main idea of the paper.

Revision tasks   (1) Ask students to reread their papers and underline the sentence(s) that explain(s) why the place was important in the family member's life. Have students whose papers lack such sentences write and add them to their paragraphs.

(2) Ask students to exchange papers with a partner and compare the partner's paper with the list of questions for "My Hometown," section 4.3 on page 70, to determine which questions have and have not been answered. Then have students write additional sentences on some or all of the questions not answered in their first drafts.

Unit 5   Describing People

5.1   *LETTER TO A HOST FAMILY:*   *Composition*   (p. 82)

Before class   Investigate and collect brochures for local host-family, day-visit, or overnight-stay programs, such as the imaginary one in the ad. They exist throughout North America and in other countries, and are often sponsored by universities and civic organizations. This activity provides an opportunity to encourage students to participate in such programs, invariably a memorable, worthwhile experience.

In class   This is not intended to be a "big" piece of work, but it is the only activity in the unit that asks students to describe themselves, a useful skill. Use it to introduce the theme of the unit and to assess students' initial proficiency. Save the first

drafts of their letters until later in the unit. When you return them for self-directed revision, refer students to recently completed activities, such as those in 5.6, "Describing Appearance and Personality," to stimulate use of more specific vocabulary.

Follow-up   Read aloud to the class some or all of the revised letters. You can "edit" the papers as you read, perhaps saving any information on physical appearance until last. As you read, have students try to guess whose paper is being read. Tell them to raise their hands as soon as they think they know and can explain the reason for their guess.

5.2   *DESCRIBING OTHER PEOPLE:*   *Dialog*   (p. 83)

Overview   The dialog in Activity A introduces in a lively fashion several easily confused questions containing the words "like" and "look like." These questions, which are commonly used to elicit descriptive information about people, are isolated for further recognition practice in Activities C and D.

Before class   Make a set of the dialog picture cues to use in class to teach the dialog. On standard-sized paper, draw your own simplified version of each frame with various colored markers. Don't be shy about your "artwork." Students will enjoy looking at it even if you don't. Or, pass out paper and markers to one or more students and have them make the class set of picture cues themselves. To save time on the day you teach the dialog, tape the six frames up on the wall or at the top of the blackboard before class or during a break.

   Fill in the blanks in the Activity A dialog with these words:
1: met, like, Does, look, like, all, look, like
2: who, look, like, see, has, curly, big, figure
3: great, What's, like, and, has, sense, humor
4: personality, does, like, music, movies, roller-
   skating, her, ankle
5: that's, is, she, much, Would, like
6: she'd, doubt, married, has, kids

In class   With students' books closed, "perform" the dialog two or three times while students *listen* carefully. Afterward, ask what they recall for each frame. Then frame by frame, teach the dialog, allowing for a lot of individual as well as group repetition. Exaggerate intonational patterns, use gestures and facial expressions, and generally "ham it up." Then have students open their books and do Activity A, filling in the missing words from memory. After you check as a group, pair students for additional practice. Show them how to cover the words and practice with the picture cues in Activity A, peeking only when absolutely necessary. For homework, assign memorization of the dialog. Tell students they will be asked to perform the dialog without reference to the words at the next class meeting. Incorporate Activities B and C at whatever point in this dialog-teaching sequence they seem appropriate. Of the five questions in Activity C, the first three are the most important for the rest of the unit. Activity D can be used in class or as homework.

5.3   SURVEY ABOUT THE TYPICAL STUDENT: *Newspaper article and thank-you letter*   (p. 85)

Before class   Ask around and find a teacher who is willing to have his or her students participate in the 15-minute interview in Activity B. If the class being interviewed is slightly more advanced than yours, both classes will get the maximum benefit – your own class because they will work hard not to embarrass themselves, and the other class because they have their reputations to maintain.

Examine the "Typical Student Survey Form" in Activity B on pages 86–7, and adapt it to your own circumstances. Then transfer the question cues on the survey form to big paper or an overhead projector transparency. You can use this display to prepare for the interviews and to tally results at the end.

In class   Have students work in pairs or small groups to make the questions for the survey form. Check as a class, using your display. As you check, have each student fill in his or her own answer to each question. It is absolutely necessary, now and in the interviews, for students to record all answers of "zero."

Before the day of the visit, get one or two volunteers to serve as class spokespersons – to introduce the class and the project to the other class, and to thank them at the close of the interview. Have a little rehearsal on the day of the visit. During the visit, have each of your students interview one member of the other class and carefully record the answers. Double up students if necessary, and consider the seating arrangement and the number of chairs needed.

There are several ways of tallying results, depending on class size. Working first in small groups and then as a class is one way. Another is to give the job to one or more volunteer "mathematicians." In any case, you will find a pocket calculator to be a real asset. Have a student with good handwriting (or one who could have good handwriting if the situation called for it) copy the final article from Activity C on a ditto mat, and make enough copies for the other class. When students write their thank-you letters to interview partners in Activity E, have them enclose a copy of the article. Choose one student to deliver all the letters at one time.

5.4   THOMAS ALVA EDISON: *Dictation*   (p. 90)

Follow the general dictation procedure in Teachers' Notes to Unit 1 on pages 125–7. As you do the various activities, keep the students focused on content. You want them to learn as much as possible about Edison in this unit, so they will be prepared for the Edison activities in Unit 6. Some classes benefit from a little test on the factual information about Edison on these pages.

Dictation quiz

Form B   From his childhood until his death, Thomas Edison asked questions constantly. He was curious about everything, but he went to school for only three months. He was a practical organizer with intense energy and determination. The almost deaf Edison was a remarkable man. (43 words)

5.6   DESCRIBING APPEARANCE AND PERSONALITY: *Spider diagram*   (p. 93)

Students really enjoy filling in the spider diagram in Activity A. It works best to begin the activity in class, so you can make sure students know what to do. Use the first word in each column as examples. Ask students to decide where each of these words belongs. When everyone agrees on the placement of the first words, let students continue the activity in pairs for a few minutes. Then ask students to finish

the spider for homework. On the following day when you check this homework orally, stop after each leg of the spider is checked and ask students to identify the nouns, if any, that can be used in the model sentence. Here are the answers to Activity A:

Build: (men) a good build, muscular; (women) a good figure, petite; (both) stocky, a medium build
Nose: crooked, pointed, wide
Skin: (color) black, brown, dark, fair; (other) wrinkles, freckles, pimples
Eyes: (color) black, brown, blue, dark, green, hazel; (kind/shape) oval, round, wide-set
Hair: (kind) curly, straight, thick, wavy; (color) auburn, black, brown, blond, dark, gray, red, salt-and-pepper; (length) short, long, medium-

length; (style – traditionally female) bangs, braids, a bun, a ponytail; (style – male) bald, a beard, a moustache, sideburns
Height: tall, short, medium-height
Overall: (male) handsome; (female) beautiful, pretty; (both) nice-looking, ordinary-looking, attractive, good-looking
Weight: medium-weight; (underweight) skinny, slender, slim, thin; (overweight) heavy, fat, chubby.

5.9 DAN'S LEAST FAVORITE DAY: *Practice text* (p. 99)

In class With students' books closed, work with the information in Figure 1. Put the vocabulary on the board, and read the definitions to the class one by one. Ask students to choose the word from the list that corresponds to each definition. Encourage related conversation whenever possible. Then dictate the first three questions in Figure 2 for students to write on a piece of scrap paper. Read

the text one or two times while students listen. Elicit the answers. Then read the text one more time. With the students' books closed, ask the last five questions in Figure 2. Finally, have students open their books and work orally through part of the Activity A sentence combining, but do not allow them to make any notes. Afterward, assign this activity as written homework.

Vocabulary	Definitions
a) change (n.)	1. place where you buy food
b) detergent	2. soap
c) dirty	3. opposite of "poor"
d) do the laundry	4. After you wash and dry the clothes, you do this (demonstrate "fold").
e) fold (v.)	
f) grocery store	5. Something costs 75¢. You pay with a dollar bill. You get 25¢ back. What is the 25¢? (Substitute local currency if necessary.)
g) hanger	
h) laundromat	
i) rich	6. opposite of "clean"
j) sort (v.)	7. place where you wash clothes
	8. to wash the clothes, towels, sheets, etc.
	9. What's this? (Draw ⌂ on board.)
	10. to separate by size, kind, color, etc.

Figure 1

1. How often does Dan need to wash his clothes?
2. What does Dan always forget to take to the laundromat?
3. What is one thing that Dan likes?
4. What does Dan hate?
5. How long does he wait to do his laundry?
6. Where does he often get change? Why?
7. Does Dan like to put his clothes on hangers?
8. If Dan gets rich, what is he going to do?

Figure 2

5.10 ACTIVE VOCABULARY PRACTICE: Silent quizzes (p. 100)

In class (1) There are three silent quizzes in the student pages. Before doing a quiz, decide the random order in which you will demonstrate the words, and put a number in the blank beside each item. When you are ready to do the quiz, simply call out each number and demonstrate the action silently. For silent quiz III, simply point to the parts of the body in random order.

(2) *"Silent" Team Tic-Tac-Toe*: Choose a Tic-Tac-Toe grid from Figure 3, and copy it on the board. Divide the class into two teams. Have the teams choose "X" and "O" and a team name, such as Lions, Tigers, Stars, etc. The students often come up with funny names. Write each team's name on the board to make a simple scoreboard. Designate a "batting order" on each team. Players cannot play out of turn. Then designate one team to go first. ("Eenie-meenie-mynie-mo / Catch-a-person-by-the-toe" is a means of designation that never fails to amuse students.)

The player whose turn it is tells you the number of a square on the tic-tac-toe grid. You say the word from that square for everyone to hear. The player silently acts out the word or points to the designated part of the body. A correct demonstration gets an "X" or an "O" in the square. The play alternates back and forth between the two teams. A right answer earns a mark, but it does not give the scoring team an additional chance to score right away. The first team to get three marks in a line horizontally, vertically, or diagonally across the grid gets a point on its scoreboard.

Although Figure 3 contains only five Tic-Tac-Toe grids, you can easily construct additional ones if the game proves to be a real hit with your class. You can display a grid with both numbers and words written in, as described above, or you can display it with only the numbers showing, the corresponding words remaining a mystery until a player chooses a particular square.

1 toes	2 throat	3 shoulders
4 chest	5 elbow	6 knees
7 chin	8 ankle	9 cheeks

1 sneeze	2 yawn	3 cough
4 whisper	5 snap	6 kick
7 count	8 whistle	9 clap

1 wink	2 bend	3 frown
4 throw	5 blink	6 jump
7 smile	8 tickle	9 shrug

1 pour	2 clap	3 chew
4 bite	5 sing	6 climb
7 fold	8 print	9 catch

1 tiptoe	2 draw	3 cry
4 shake	5 hit	6 scratch
7 fly	8 wave	9 hug

Figure 3

Additional actions Here is an alphabetical list for your inspiration as you plan AVP activities for this unit.

Blow up a balloon. Pop it.	Pick up the receiver. /	Take a piece of gum out of
Blink. (The sun is too	Listen for the dial tone. /	your pocket. / Unwrap it.
bright.)	Dial the number. (Bzzt.	/ Put the wrapper in your
Bite your nails (fingernails).	Bzzt. It's busy!) / Frown.	pocket. / Put the gum in
Bend down (over).	/ Put down the receiver.	your mouth. / Chew it. /
Bend your knees (elbow,	Point to someone wearing	Blow a bubble. / Pop it.
foot, thumb).	red shoes (a black shirt,	Tell a secret. / Whisper.
Cross your legs (arms).	a striped skirt, etc.).	Throw the ball. / Catch it. /
Clap 3 times.	Put your thumbs up	Kick the ball.
Climb the stairs (a ladder).	(thumbs down, one	Tickle your ribs. / Laugh!
Cough. / Sneeze. / Take a	thumb up and one down).	Tiptoe. (Shhh!)
pill. / Swallow.	Raise your eyebrows (one	Try to reach the ceiling.
Count the lights (students,	eyebrow).	Whisper "hello." (Shhh!
desks, briefcases, etc.).	(Bzzzz. A mosquito bit	The baby is asleep.)
Draw a cat.	you!) Scratch the bite	Whistle "Happy Birthday."
Frown. / Smile. / Laugh. /	(your nose, head).	Wiggle your ears (fingers,
Cry.	Shake your head "no."	toes). (NOTE: especially
Jump 2 times.	Shrug your shoulders.	good if the teacher can
Make a fist. / Shake your	Sing "Happy Birthday."	demonstrate.)
fist. (You're very	Snap your fingers 2 times.	Yawn.
angry.)	Stand on your tiptoes.	

5.11 FAMILY HISTORY PROJECT – PERSONAL DESCRIPTION: Composition (p. 100)

Overview Students' finished papers in Activity C should contain three types of information about their family members: physical appearance, personality, and interests. Since all three are to be described in a single paragraph, students must choose their family members' most prominent characteristics in each domain and devote approximately one third of their paragraph to each. For help in describing physical appearance, both overall and specific, students can be referred to the spider diagram on page 94. As a basis for describing personality and interests, students should be urged to use their ideas and sentences from Activities A and B.

Revision tasks (1) Focus students' attention on the idea of balanced paragraph development. Ask students to count the number of words and/or sentences they used to convey each of the three types of information: personality, interests, and appearance. Then, after discussing what percentage of the paragraph should be devoted to each, have the students add or delete information in

appropriate places to achieve these percentages.

(2) To encourage students to analyze the content of their work, have them exchange papers and "test" whether their partners' papers contain answers to the questions in Figure 4. Authors might, if necessary, point out to their partners any information they might have overlooked. Any

1. What did the person look like?
   a. overall: ....
   b. detail 1: ....
   c. detail 2: ....

2. What did the person like to do?
   a. ....
   b. ....

3. What was the person like?
   a. strength: ....
   b. weakness: ....

Figure 4

paragraph that fails to provide this minimum amount of information is underdeveloped and needs information added in certain spots. A more sophisticated "test" might also require students to

identify supporting evidence for the traits and interests listed in the second and third questions in Figure 4.

SPECIAL ACTIVITY: *Four-piece story puzzle*

Overview On pages 176–178 are twelve pictures, arranged in random order. When these pictures are cut out, sorted, and put in correct order, they form three picture compositions, each consisting of four pictures. You will use only one of the three picture compositions, the one about a frustrating trip to the laundromat, in this information-gap writing activity. (The two remaining picture compositions are used in the special activity described in the Teachers' Notes to Unit 6 on page 164.) You can schedule this activity any time after students have completed "Dan's Least Favorite Day" (5.9 on p. 99), so they can draw on its laundry-related vocabulary.

This activity is fun and challenging to students because it has several "puzzle," or information-gap, elements: The picture composition is presented in pieces; the pieces are not in order; and no one has access to all four pieces. Each student starts with only one piece of the puzzle. That is, each student gets to see only one of the four pictures. To figure out the whole story, he or she has to get information about the other three pictures from classmates.

Creating an atmosphere of secrecy and a spirit of group cooperation is the key to success in this activity as well as the special activity in Unit 6. If you did not (or could not) remove the picture pages from your students' books earlier in the course, BE SURE to have students put away their books before you begin. DO NOT let students use their books during the activity, and DO NOT mention or in any other way draw attention to the fact that the pictures are in the book. If students are alerted to the picture pages, some may end up studying all twelve pictures after class and, therefore, find the special activity in Unit 6 less challenging and enjoyable than it might otherwise have been.

Before class (1) Prepare a set of pictures by cutting out the four laundromat pictures. (If your class is much larger than sixteen, you will need two sets of the four pictures instead of just one set.) You can either remove the pictures from your students' books or make photocopies of the pictures in your book. Mount each picture on a

standard-sized piece of paper for easier handling by the students. Note that the square, triangle, rectangle, or circle that appears in the upper right-hand corner of each picture will make it easier to identify and refer to the pictures individually.

(2) Prepare the true-false quizzes and answer keys in Figure 5 on the next page. There are one quiz and one key per picture. Simply copy the statements and answers onto separate index cards or small papers that you can hand out at the designated time. (Tell students NOT to write on the pictures or other materials so that you can use them again.)

Step 1: Working with only one picture (1) Divide students into four groups. With grand secrecy, hand out the four pictures, giving each group only one picture. Tell the groups they have one minute to study their picture and prepare for a quiz.

(2) At the end of the minute, have the groups cover up their picture. Give each group one copy of the true-false quiz on their picture. Tell them to work together and reach agreement on the correct answers before asking you for the answer key. After they have checked their answers against the answer key, let the groups uncover their picture and look at it again. Collect the quizzes and answer keys, but let each group keep their picture.

(3) Ask each group to write a description of their picture. Display the directions in Figure 6 on the next page as a guide. Students in each group should work together, but each person must write the group's description on his or her own paper (for use in Step 2). When the groups have finished writing, collect all the pictures and put them out of sight.

Step 2: Putting together the story (1) Put students into new groups, each of which must contain at least one student from each of the four original groups.

(2) Tell the new groups they must figure out the order of the pictures and the story the pictures tell. Because only one or maybe two students in each new group will be able to describe a particular picture, they will have to inform the rest of the

True-False Quizzes on Individual Laundromat Pictures

Copy each quiz on an index card or small paper.

■ 1. Folded clothes were on the table.
2. It was 3 p.m.
3. A young man in jeans and a striped sweater was putting clothes into a washing machine.
4. Dryers cost 45¢.
5. Some clothes were hanging on clothes hangers, and some clothes were in a cart.

● 1. It was 9 p.m.
2. There was a pizza restaurant next door to the laundromat.
3. A young man in jeans and a striped sweater was carrying a basket of clothes.
4. More clothes were in the back of the young man's car.
5. No one was inside the laundromat because it was closed.

▲ 1. Dryers cost 50¢.
2. It was about 5:30.
3. A young man in jeans and a striped sweater was putting money into a dryer.
4. Three people were putting clothes into washing machines.
5. One person was taking a basket of folded clothes out of the laundromat.

■ 1. The laundromat was open.
2. A young man in jeans and a striped sweater was carrying a basket of clothes into the laundromat.
3. It was 2 p.m.
4. Someone in a car splashed water on the young man and his basket of clothes.
5. The young man looked surprised.

Answers

Copy each set of answers on an index card or paper.

■		▲		●		■	
1.	T	1.	F	1.	F	1.	F
2.	F	2.	T	2.	F	2.	F
3.	F	3.	T	3.	T	3.	F
4.	T	4.	F	4.	T	4.	T
5.	T	5.	T	5.	F	5.	T

Figure 5

a) Tell what happened and *when*.
b) Tell about the person or people:
   – Describe his/her/their physical appearance.
   – What was she / was he / were they wearing?
                                                doing?
                                                feeling?
c) Tell about the place.

Figure 6

group about it. To do this, students can take turns reading aloud and answering questions about the descriptions they wrote in the original groups.

(3) Have one student from each group tell the whole class the group's version of the story. Finally, to confirm the accuracy of the stories and satisfy curiosity, show the class the four pictures in the correct order.

Step 3: Finishing the story   Draw the diagram in Figure 7, which represents the picture composition, on the board. Ask students to imagine a picture 5. Elicit and list several ideas for possible endings, at least one of which must be "happy."

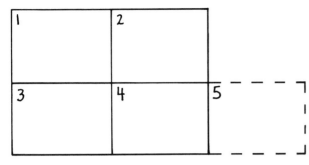

Figure 7

Step 4: Writing from a point of view

Introduce this letter-writing activity by telling students an anecdote in which a person, perhaps yourself, turns a bad or frustrating incident in his or her life into a humorous, entertaining story. Have students, working individually, take the role of the principal character in the picture composition and write a letter. In the letter they must include the story in pictures 1–4 plus an ending (one of the suggestions for picture 5). Before they start writing, talk about who they will write to and what, besides the story, they will include to fill out the letter.

Step 5: Sharing the stories (1) Choose one of the better letters, edit it, and have the author record it on tape to use as a dictation. Use this dictation exercise with the class as a whole or with small groups on a day when you want to have two or three simultaneous activities. Since all students will be generally familiar with the content of the letter, they should be able to understand their classmate's pronunciation in the tape-recorded dictation.

(2) Choose one of the better letters, edit it, and have the author copy it correctly on a ditto mat. Duplicate the letter, and have each student write a letter in reply for homework or buffer work.

(3) Read some of the letters aloud to the class and ask which ending sounds best.

Unit 6   Describing People's Lives

6.1   *HALEY'S FAMILY HISTORY PROJECT: Dictation*   (p. 103)

Follow the general dictation procedure in the Teachers' Notes to Unit 1 on pages 125–7.

Dictation quiz

Form B   <u>Roots</u> is a historical novel that American author Alex Haley wrote about 200 years of his family history. The story begins with Kunta Kinte, Haley's great-great-great-great-grandfather, who was kidnapped from Africa in 1767 to be sold in America as a slave. A few of Kinte's African words were in Haley's family for seven generations. Eventually, they helped Haley discover Kinte's tribal origin in western Africa. (65 words)

6.2   *REVISING: "Edison's Most Famous Invention"*   (p. 104)

Overview   The facts about Edison and his invention of the light bulb, which are contained in the lecture in Figure 1, are important not only in this section but also in section 6.3, "Working with a Biography: Edison." You should therefore handle these activities thoroughly and encourage students to master the facts presented in the lecture.

Activity A   (1) The lecture for Activity A is in Figure 1. Before beginning the lecture, get students ready to listen carefully by previewing the questions in Activity A. Elicit their ideas about what kinds of information they expect to hear during the lecture. Then have students close their books and get out a clean sheet of paper for notetaking. Discuss why notetaking is useful (improves concentration and comprehension, serves as study and/or memory aid, etc.); what kinds of things to write (words, numbers, and phrases instead of sentences); how to arrange information in notes (numbering ideas or parts of the lecture, leaving blank lines to separate ideas, writing fewer words per line, making vertical lists when appropriate; and whether spelling or other mistakes in notes are important.

(2) Tell students to write as many notes as possible and leave space for any information they miss. Using a natural, conversational style, read the lecture aloud two, three, or even four times, depending on the skills of your students, and insist students add to their notes during each repetition. Then ask students to open their books to Activity A and use their notes to answer the questions. Check orally, pausing after each answer for a show of hands on who answered correctly and whose notes contain the answer. If you plan to wait a while before doing Activities B and C, be sure you have students file these lecture notes in their notebooks for safekeeping because they will be needed in the later activities.

Activity A Lecture: Edison's Most Important Invention

Thomas Edison wanted to find a practical way to change electricity into light. He thought that it was possible to do this. He had started to experiment with electricity when he was very young. By August 1878, when he began his experiments with light, Edison was 37 years old. Because he had already had more than fifteen years of experience with electricity, he had some good ideas about how to make light from an electric current.

Edison experimented for over two years before he was completely successful. His first problem was oxygen. There is oxygen in the air. When air, and therefore oxygen, is present, materials will burn easily. Edison didn't want his material to burn; he wanted it to get very hot and glow brightly when electricity passed through it. In other words, he wanted it to make light without fire. Edison finally solved this problem. He put his material, called a filament, inside a glass bulb. Then he took all the air out and made a vacuum inside the glass bulb. There is nothing in a vacuum, not air, not oxygen, not anything. In the vacuum, the filament got very hot when electricity passed through it, but the filament could not burn because there was no oxygen present.

Edison's second and more difficult problem was to find the right material for the filament. The filament is the small, thin piece of material inside the glass bulb. It is the filament that glows and gives light. For the filament, Edison needed a material that did not melt when electricity passed through it. In other words, he needed a material with a high melting point. He tried platinum. Platinum worked, but not very well. Also, it was not practical because it was too expensive. So, Edison did more experiments. He tested thousands of materials. He tried every material in his laboratory. Nothing worked. One day he even tried using a red hair from the beard of a friend. It didn't work either. He sent people to foreign countries looking for special materials that he wanted to try. For example, he sent people to the forests of Japan and the jungles near the Amazon River looking for bamboo.

Finally, in October 1879, after 14 months of experiments, he tried a carbonized thread. He charred some ordinary cotton sewing thread. In other words, he heated the thread until it became black like charcoal. Then he passed an electric current through it. It glowed for 40 hours. The carbonized thread filament worked well because it had a high melting point and was not very expensive. It was in this way that the first practical electric light bulb was made. But the bulb was still not ready for commercial production. That is, it was not ready to make in large quantities and sell in stores. Edison worked for over a year and finally made bulbs to sell. The bulbs had filaments of carbonized bamboo.

Modern electric light bulbs are not exactly the same as Edison's first bulbs; they are better than Edison's. Modern bulbs have filaments made of a metal called tungsten. Modern bulbs also come in more sizes and last much longer. Edison's first bulb lasted only 40 hours. The average life of a modern light bulb is 1,000 hours or more. Also, Edison made a vacuum inside his first light bulb. Today nitrogen and argon are inside light bulbs, but there is still no oxygen present. But, even today, Edison's main idea is still used. So, when we turn on a light today, we should remember Thomas Edison. Edison was the great inventor who gave light to the world.

Figure 1

Activities B and C   These activities focus on the importance of factual accuracy in academic writing. Emphasize that there are no grammatical mistakes in the summary and that students should focus only on the facts. If your students enjoy competition, you can organize the search for factual mistakes in Activity B as a contest among pairs or small groups of students.

6.3   WORKING WITH A BIOGRAPHY: *Edison*   (p. 107)

Overview   This is the first of four sections that deal with biographical compositions. While the later sections, 6.4 ("Personality Profile"), 6.8 ("Family History Project – Short biography"), and 6.9 ("Family History Project – Final paper") involve students in organizing and actually writing compositions, the structured activities in this section are intended to introduce them to how an outline looks and how information in an outline can be put into sentence and paragraph form in a composition. The facts needed to complete the outline in Activity A can be found in 3.6 ("Edison's Typical Working Day"), 5.4 ("Thomas Alva Edison"), and 6.2 ("Edison's Most Famous Invention"). If you have skipped any of these sections, you should have students do them, at least in an abbreviated fashion, before beginning these activities.)

In class   Introduce Activity A by discussing what a biography is. Then discuss with students the format and content of the outline. Also, point out that question marks (?) indicate blanks to be filled. Do not, however, say anything about where to find information for the blanks. Most students will realize, as soon as they begin the activity, that they need to do some "research" in their books and notebooks to locate the missing facts. When you check Activity A with your students, make sure they not only have the correct answers in the blanks but also understand the rest of the information in the outline. Begin Activity B by asking the questions in the student pages. These questions will focus students' attention on the relationship between the outline in Activity A and the composition in the box. Then ask students to read the first paragraph and fill in the blanks. Tell them to use good grammar and correct spelling in their answers. Check the first paragraph before assigning the rest.

6.4   PERSONALITY PROFILE: *Composition/newspaper activity*   (p. 110)

Overview   This sequence of activities always sparks interest and motivation among students because everyone wants to perform well in the presence of the visitor you invite to class. It is also an essential intermediate step between the Edison biography and the students' own biographies of their family members in the Family History Project in Section 6.8.

Before class   (1) Well in advance, find a fluent English speaker who is willing to come to your class and spend about 45 minutes being interviewed. The best guest is an English speaker who works in your school but does not have prolonged daily contact with your students. The administrator of your program is an especially good choice because both administrator and students welcome an opportunity to talk with each other about something other than problems. If such an in-house guest is not available, invite any other English speaker you can locate. If possible, involve students in extending a formal invitation and finalizing the date, whether in person, by phone, or in a letter.

(2) Review the interview questions in Activity A, and adjust them as necessary to suit the life of your guest. If you are not at all familiar with your guest's background, be sure to ask for a brief overview ahead of time.

(3) Look through magazines and newspapers, especially the Sunday supplement, for some personality/celebrity profiles. Cut out several you can use in class to introduce this sequence of activities.

In class   After students have prepared interview questions in Activity A and used them to interview you in Activity B, write up and hand out a profile of yourself, that is, a composition about your life based on the information you gave students in the interview. Use the third-person singular throughout the profile, referring to yourself as "he" or "she." Include in your profile 15 FACTUAL mistakes. For homework ask students to find and correct these mistakes with the help of their interview notes. This homework assignment, which is not mentioned in the student pages, is effective in showing students how information from an interview can be transformed into a composition.

Before your class undertakes Activity C, you need to take care of several procedural matters that will make the interview of the visitor go smoothly. First, decide with your students' help who is going to ask which question(s) from Activity A during the interview. To give the interview a natural feeling, assign the questions to students with an eye to their

seating arrangement so that successive questions come from students in different parts of the room. Second, to make sure there is time for all the assigned questions, tell students to wait until the end of the interview to ask any extra questions that might occur to them. Finally, spend some time with your students on the pronunciation of any words or questions that prove to be troublesome.

Follow-up   A thank-you letter to your guest is a must. Guide the class in drafting one on the board. Have one student copy it neatly on unlined paper. Get everyone's signature before sending or delivering it. Or, have everyone make a neat final copy and choose the best-looking one to send.

6.6   *ACTIVE VOCABULARY PRACTICE:* *Verb review*   (p. 113)

Before assigning either of the exercises, display the vocabulary list that precedes them and act out the words with your students. In a subsequent class session, display the list again and, with students' books closed, do an oral exercise loosely based on the information in Exercises A and B. Here are some examples.

Q: When do you *blink*?
A: When the sun is in my eyes.

Q: When do you *blow a bubble*?
A: When I chew bubble gum.

After you have asked a few example questions, have students take over the questioning.

6.7   *FAMILY HISTORY PROJECT – SIGNIFICANT EVENT: Composition*   (p. 114)

Overview   The paragraph that students write in Activity B may turn out to be longer than earlier pieces of this project. It will, however, probably be easy for students to write. By now students have had a lot of experience with storytelling, and narration presents few organization problems. Students will also enjoy writing this piece and come up with some interesting, amazing tales to tell and write.

Revision tasks   If you have not already attempted peer revision and editing activities, now is the time. Have students exchange papers and read their partners' paper twice – first to see if they have any problems understanding the story, and again to check if all verbs are in the past tense. Tell students to circle the problems they find.

6.8   *FAMILY HISTORY PROJECT – SHORT BIOGRAPHY: Composition*   (p. 115)

Before class   Copy the 28 outline items in Activity A on strips of paper and scramble them in an envelope. Then copy the four headings, which are in the box, on small index cards or on different colored strips of paper, and put them in the same envelope. Actually, you can use any system that makes it apparent which items are the headings.

Prepare an envelope of strips for every two to four students in the class.

Activity A   Form students into pairs or small groups, and distribute the envelopes. Have each group remove the headings and lay them out in order on the floor or any large surface. Tell students to remove the strips one at a time and decide under which heading each one belongs. (A few of them can be logically placed under more than one heading.) Circulate and assist. When the students have succeeded in grouping related strips, ask them to arrange the strips in each group in biographical order. Again, variation is possible. Finally, have each student make a copy of the finished outline for future reference.

Activity B   Refer students to the fact sheet in Unit 2 on page 42 and to all previous Family History Project activities and compositions. They should be able to find most but not all of the information called for by the outline items. Don't expect a perfect, complete outline from any but the ablest class members. All students, however, will need to produce some kind of chronological list or outline to use in writing the short biography.

Activity C   This paper is long but not too difficult for students to write. Students will need to

work on it in more than one class session or begin it in class and finish it at home. It should contain at least four paragraphs, be written in the past tense, and be packed with as many year, age, and duration facts as possible.

Revision tasks   Have students add dates, ages, and durational information (e.g., "for 20 years") at appropriate places throughout their papers. In particular, have them check the first sentence of each paragraph to see if it contains this type of information. Then show students how to string together a lot of data in single sentences, perhaps as complex as these:

- In 1915, when my grandfather was 30 years old, he married my grandmother, who was 20.
- My grandmother taught school for 40 years before she retired in 1960 at the age of 65.
- In 1950, after 50 years of marriage, my uncle died and my aunt lived alone for the next five years.

6.9   *FAMILY HISTORY PROJECT – FINAL PAPER: Composition*   (p. 116)

Overview   Once students grasp the basic concept of how to integrate several papers into one long composition, planning and writing the final paper is relatively easy. But because students will need to work several hours at a stretch to do this, spend class time discussing the process and assign the actual writing as homework.

Once the final paper is turned in, handle it differently than you handled the shorter pieces. Treat it as a final product. Tell students that you will read and grade it as it is. In this instance, forego any revision or editing not only because of practical time constraints, but also because this is the way final papers are handled in content courses.

Regardless of how imperfect the final papers may be, rest assured that the experience of writing them will pay off for your students in the future. For now, students know the satisfaction and pride that comes from producing a lengthy body of work of some lasting significance to themselves and others.

Before class   (1) Several days ahead, check students' Family History Project folders (or have students check their own notebooks) to see that all their earlier pieces are in a corrected final form. If any piece is missing or incomplete, have the student replace or recopy it.

(2) Look at all the papers that one of your

students has written. Put yourself in his or her shoes. Mentally go through the process of integrating the pieces into a final paper. Use the insights you gain to plan a class discussion of the integration process.

(3) Reread your students' "first thoughts" papers from Unit 2. Look for and underline all the "good" ideas, phrases, and words that students can use in writing the introduction and conclusion of the final papers. Also, watch for and mark important facts that students failed to include in the short biography.

In class   (1) Copy the diagram in Activity B on the board. Explain to students that each block represents a paragraph, with the middle four blocks corresponding to their four-paragraph "short biography" from section 6.8. Discuss with them where in their short biography they should insert the other paragraphs they have written, and how they should go about inserting them. For example, the Unit 3 "routine day" paragraph belongs with the "childhood and early years" paragraph. To integrate these two paragraphs, students will probably have to divide the childhood and early years paragraph and rewrite some sentences so they can function as first sentences of a new paragraph. These two paragraphs, when combined, might become three separate paragraphs. Once students understand the basic idea, have them sketch out a plan for integrating their pieces.

(2) Return students' first-thoughts papers. Tell them you have marked the good parts, not the bad parts. Tell them these papers contain some good ideas for their introductions and conclusions. Have them reread the papers and begin writing the introduction in class.

Follow-up When you return your students' final papers, discuss how they will share them with other people in their families. Encourage them to make a copy and mail it home soon. If no one in the family reads English, perhaps they could prepare and send a translation as well. Also, discuss some concrete, feasible ways in which they can preserve the paper for future readers. Some of these ways might include putting it in a family photo album, in a box of important family documents and mementos, or even in a family safe or safe-deposit box.

SPECIAL ACTIVITY: *The great story-writing contest*

Overview Among the 12 pictures on pages 176–178 you will find eight pictures that can be arranged into two picture stories, or compositions – a set of four pictures about a surprise party and another set about a rotten morning. These two picture compositions are the stimulus for a story-writing contest in which the students themselves choose the winners.

Before class (1) To prepare for Step 1, make enough four-picture sets so that half of your students will each receive the four "rotten-morning" pictures and the other half will each get the four "surprise-party" pictures. (You can either remove the pictures from your students' books or make photocopies of the pictures in your book.) Simply clip the four pictures together, and have individuals lay them out in order before using them. Or, time permitting, mount each set on a piece of paper for easier handling.

(2) Make "A" name tags to identify half of your students and "B" name tags for the other half by writing "A" or "B" on small pieces of paper. Students will need these taped or pinned on during Steps 1 and 2.

(3) Make copies of the two tests in Figure 2 so that half of the students will receive one test and half will receive the other in Step 3.

(4) Devise prizes (e.g., certificates, ribbons, trinkets, books) for the winners in the contest explained in Step 5. The prizes can be nice or merely mock serious, for example, a certificate saying "to the best level-two story writer in this part of the world."

Step 1: Preparing to tell a story Divide the class into two groups, A and B, and have students put on their tags. With grand "secrecy" give a "surprise party" picture set to each student in A and a "rotten morning" picture set to each student in B. Tell students that they will have 15 minutes to prepare to tell, but not read, their respective stories to a member of the *other* group. Allow students to use their dictionaries, ask you questions, make notes, and write out sentences to help them get ready, but tell them they must put aside their notes and pictures at the end of the preparation period. At first let them work alone if they wish, but before the preparation period is over, have them practice telling the story at least twice to someone else in their own group. For classes that need some guidance, display the directions in Figure 6 (p. 158) in the Teachers' Notes to Unit 5.

Step 2: Telling the stories This fast-paced step, which packs a lot of student interaction into a short amount of time, consists of three story-exchange periods during which each student will work with three partners, one at a time, from the other group. In other words, each A will work with a series of three B's, and each B will work with a series of three A's. During each story-exchange period the partners are given a short time in which to "tell/teach" their story and then "listen to/learn" their partner's story. Students may NOT use any pictures or notes during this process, so collect all materials or have students put them completely out of sight before you begin.

To ensure a quick and orderly change of partners each time, have students sit or stand in a circle with A's and B's alternating. (If you have an odd number of students, you must join the circle and assume the role of A or B.) A's will *always* work with the B on their right. To change partners each time, the B's stay in place while the A's move one

Tests on the two stories

Party

1. The story was about
   a) a teenager.
   b) a middle-aged woman.
   c) a little girl.
2. At the beginning of the story, she was
   a) cheerful.
   b) not too bright.
   c) upset.
3. Family and friends were decorating
   a) the yard for a birthday party.
   b) a Christmas tree.
   c) the room for a small party.

4. The room was dark and quiet because
   a) the party was a surprise.
   b) there was no electricity.
   c) no one was using it.
5. At the party there weren't any
   a) presents.
   b) balloons.
   c) people with frowns.

Morning

1. This story was about
   a) a teenager.
   b) an adult.
   c) a man in his eighties.
2. He had a Band-Aid on his jaw because
   a) he was sick.
   b) the dog bit him.
   c) he cut himself while shaving.
3. He burned the toast, and the coffee spilled
   a) on his briefcase.
   b) on the floor.
   c) on his shirt.

4. In this story there weren't any
   a) alarm clocks.
   b) wet newspapers.
   c) taxis on duty.
5. At the end of this story this person was
   a) upset.
   b) ambitious.
   c) cheerful.

Figure 2

position to the right. After each move, the A's will each have a new B partner on their right.

(1) When the students are in position in a circle, begin the first story-exchange period by writing on the board "A's talk; B's listen." Tell the class that each A will have one minute to tell his or her story to the B on his or her right. Start the minute dramatically with "Get ready; get set; go!" Adjust the "minute" so that most students are just finishing when you say "Stop." Then write "B's talk; A's listen" and start another "minute" during which students continue working with the same partners but reverse roles.

(2) Change partners for the second story-exchange period by having the A's move one position to the right as explained above. Repeat "A's talk; B's listen" but announce only 50 seconds. Then "B's talk; A's listen" for 50 more seconds.

(3) For the third period, change partners by once again having the A's move to the right. Repeat the two talking and listening periods for 45 seconds each.

Step 3: Testing (1) Regroup A's together on their side of the room and B's together on their side. Have A's tell each other the stories they *heard* while B's do the same.

(2) Give each student a test about the story that he or she heard. Check the tests. Total the number of correct answers among the A's and then among the B's to see which group scored better and which group "taught" better. Finally, let everyone see both sets of pictures.

Step 4: Writing expanded stories for the contest

Put the diagram in Figure 3 on the board. Tell students that the numbers 1 through 4 represent the four pictures in each story. Ask students to write down, but not share, ideas for a new beginning (picture 0) and a new ending (picture 5) for *both* the rotten morning and the surprise party stories. Tell students that they must each write a story for "the great story-writing contest." Tell them they may choose either of the two basic stories, but they must expand the story they select by adding a new ending and a new beginning. Tell the students that their expanded stories will be judged by other students on these points: creative beginning, creative ending, accurate information in the body, interesting details, and attractive format and appearance.

Collect the finished stories and mark the surface errors in grammar and mechanics with editing symbols. Do not, however, revise the content or the organization of the stories. Return the marked papers to the students to put into final form for the contest, but do not give specific directions concerning the final format except to require that students' names be written on the back of the paper, not the front.

Step 5: Conducting the contest

While there are other ways of conducting "the great story-writing contest," the particular method explained here contains several procedures specifically intended to enable your class to complete the contest in a reasonable amount of time. The reasoning behind these procedures will be apparent if you consider two important points. First, the fastest and easiest way to determine winners is simply to add up the scores for each story, but addition will work only if each story is scored by the same number of students. If the number of scores per story were to vary, you would have to resort to averaging the scores, a more time-consuming process of determining the winners. Second, the more times a story is scored, the more class time the scoring and tallying will consume. While all students in a class of perhaps three to six students can read and score all stories in a reasonable amount of time, a larger class cannot. This time problem can be solved by limiting the number of student scores per story to four, which produces a fair evaluation in a reasonably short time without unduly limiting student participation.

⟫→

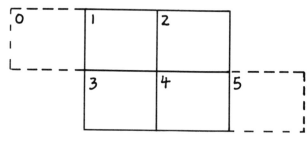

Figure 3

Story contest score card

** ENTRY NUMBER ____ **

Circle one number per line.

	Poor	Fair	Average	Good	Excellent
1. Creative beginning	1	2	3	4	5
2. Creative ending	1	2	3	4	5
3. Accurate information in the body	1	2	3	4	5
4. Interesting details	1	2	3	4	5
5. Attractive format & appearance	1	2	3	4	5

** TOTAL SCORE ____ **

Your name: ....

Figure 4

(1) Number the stories in the contest, and make score cards (Figure 4). Determine how many score cards are needed by multiplying the number of stories by four. Either photocopy the score card in Figure 4, or write it on the board and have students make the required number of copies.

(2) Post the stories around the room, and hand out the score cards to students. If the number of stories and the number of students present on the day of the contest are the same, give each student four score cards. Otherwise, divide the score cards among the students as evenly as possible.

(3) Tell students they will circulate around the room to read and score the stories using one of their score cards per story. Explain that, because each story is to be scored only four times, they must put a checkmark ($\checkmark$) in the lower left-hand corner of each story that they score. When a story has four checkmarks, its scoring is complete. While all students should be encouraged to read all stories, either during or after the contest, be sure they understand they must not fill out another score card on a story that already has four checkmarks.

(4) Collect the score cards. Have students tally the scores to determine winners by adding up the four scores for each story. You might ask for two or three volunteers to handle the job. Announce the winners, and award the prizes. Read the winning stories to the class, or ask the prize-winning authors to do so.

WRITING SAMPLE   (Unit 1, p. 4)

If your students did a writing sample with the bank robbery pictures in Section 1.4, and you saved them as suggested, now is the time for follow-up. Without any warning, have students write the story again. Collect their papers, and look them over. On the following day, which should be the last or almost the last class session, return both versions. Point out to students how much progress they have made, and congratulate them. Then have them stand up, stretch, and give themselves a round of applause.

Appendixes

Appendix 1: Creating a Class Newspaper

MAKING OVERALL PLANS

Glance at the two pages from a sample class newspaper on pages 172–173. Then quickly flip through *all* the newspaper activities in the book to get a sense of the whole project. *Your* calendar of events, rather than the sequence of units in the book, may determine the best time for scheduling some of them. In particular, you will need to make arrangements for the class trip (Unit 4), the survey about the typical student (Unit 5), and the personality profile interview (Unit 6). These activities, which put students in contact with people from outside the class, generate considerable student interest and are well worth a little advance planning. Also, decide when you want to "publish" the newspaper. You may want to do two or three small issues or one elaborate one. Set deadlines accordingly.

CHOOSING A FORMAT

Individual copies How you "publish" your class newspaper depends on facilities and circumstances. If at all possible, arrange to make a copy for each student in the class and enough extras for the students' other teachers and school administrators. Photocopying the paper is easier than duplicating it by ditto or mimeo. If your school cannot afford the photocopying, perhaps the students can pay for their own copies.

Single display copy If you cannot make individual copies, make one copy and display it prominently, just as in earlier times newspapers were posted for everyone to pass by and read. Either type the display newspaper or make a more readable display by making a "giant" newspaper with articles, headlines, and graphics handwritten by students. Have an "unveiling ceremony" at the publication reception described on page 171.

LAYING OUT THE NEWSPAPER

Basic procedure The basic procedure is simple. Type or write the articles in columns. Cut out the columns, arrange them attractively on pages (or posterboard), and stick them down. Write in headlines, and fill in the blank spaces with drawings, graphs, cartoons, acknowledgments, and "ads." When laying out the front page, attach columns to one of the student-designed masthead pages from Activity E in section 1.10.

Student participation Enlist as much student help as possible in the layout process, either before, during, or after class. Also, include as many different individuals as possible. Any one student should not work on everything because the finished newspaper should have some surprises to make it more interesting to read. Emphasize participation rather than perfection. The layout is rich with opportunities to give less talented language learners a sense of positive personal involvement in something associated with their English class.

Preliminary layout   If time permits, devote a class session to preliminary layout. First, look at commercial papers and newsletters. Talk about where different types of articles go in a paper and what makes a page attractive. Then put students to work with scissors, rulers, pencils, small markers, tape, blank paper, copies of articles typed in columns *without* headlines (one set of articles for each pair of students), and a list of headlines. If some students are floundering, help them decide what will go on each page, but not in what arrangement. Try to leave them with enough freedom to develop their own ideas. Collect the students' papers for ideas and artwork to use in the final layout.

Final layout   If you don't have class time for preliminary layouts, arrange the articles and attach them to pages. Take the pages to class, and have a variety of students print in the headlines and page headings, and add the artwork. In making the final layout, you can use ordinary cellophane tape, even masking tape, or almost any kind of paste or glue; however, double-stick tape and/or a glue stick are more convenient to use.

Double-sided layout   Lay out the newspaper to be printed on both sides of the page if you can. Such an arrangement looks more authentic and allows double-page spreads. If double-sided copying is not feasible, you can achieve a double-sided effect. Just have students staple or tape pages together with blank sides back to back before they staple the whole paper together.

PREPARING ARTICLES FOR LAYOUT

Typing   Try to get selections in final form as you go to avoid a last-minute rush. Type them in columns as soon as you can. If possible, have students type and proofread them. Take a portable typewriter to be used in a corner somewhere. Or, arrange for student access to a machine already on the premises.

Column size   When typing selections for layout, set the margins to make columns 3½ inches wide, and use a guide sheet. To make one, just take a clean sheet of typing paper and draw two heavy vertical lines 3½ inches apart with a dark marker. Put the guide sheet into the machine behind the page you are typing, and keep your typing between the lines.

Cloze format   Type at least one selection per issue with blanks every 7th word or so. In this format the selection serves as a cloze exercise in the class session devoted to reading the paper. Particularly good choices for this treatment are articles that all of the students have worked on.

Headlines   Have students write headlines as the articles are produced. Start by giving students several headlines to choose from. Discuss why some are better than others. Build to students' writing headlines themselves if possible.

MAKING ILLUSTRATIONS

Drawings   Since the class newspaper is by and for the students, drawings made by students of themselves and other classmates are easy and appropriate decorations. As a quick exercise in following directions, similar to Active Vocabulary Practice, ask students to draw two squares, each approximately one inch by one inch. In one square have them draw their own faces, and in the other square the face of a student of the opposite sex. During this activity, chuckles and interaction among the students are guaranteed. Collect the drawings, and use them to decorate "Meet the Class" or "In Search of the Typical Student." Or, use them as borders or as fillers throughout the paper.

Advertisements   "Ads" stimulate creativity and fun. Have students design advertisements to promote travel to their cities or countries. Or, specify ads for instant and preposterous study aids such as TOEFL pills, grammar injections, and perfect-English pencils.

»»→

Cartoons   To make cartoons, show students a few examples of cartoons and comics from newspapers and magazines. Then display some frames from which you have deleted the captions, and have students write their own captions. Discuss aspects of the students' common situation that might serve as inspiration for cartoons. List the ideas generated, and have artistic students develop the pictures.

Graphs   Graphs are great for bringing math, geography, etc., into the English class. Show examples of different kinds of graphs from newspapers, magazines, or textbooks. Copy (or have a student copy) one or two simple graphs on a transparency or big paper. Prepare questions, true-false statements, and/or fill-ins over these samples. Finally, have one to three interested students make their own graphs. Nationalities of students in the English program or their native languages are possible topics.

EXPANDING THE CONTENTS OF THE NEWSPAPER

Interviews   Have students interview other students in the school who have participated in events, trips, or homestays arranged by the English program. If you are teaching in a non-English-speaking country and some students have visited English-speaking countries, have student "reporters" interview the "travelers" for reports on their visits.

Reports on school events   Have students collect information and write reports on upcoming or past English-program or school events.

Horoscope   Create a feature called "Your Ideal Horoscope." First, have students read horoscopes taken from commercial newspapers and magazines and answer questions about them. If possible, also record a telephone horoscope and bring it to class for transcription or listening cloze. Then ask students to write "ideal" predictions and advice for their individual astrological signs. In other words, have them write what they would like to read (predictions) or what they need to read (advice). Compile the predictions and advice into the form of a horoscope for publication.

Advice column   (1) Select two or three advice columns from commercial newspapers and

magazines, and condense each problem letter into a single question. Then ask students to read the columns, determine which letters state problems and which letters give advice, and match the condensations with the problem letters. (2) Have students work in small groups or pairs to write their own problem letters. Suggest that they write about typical problems of students or use their humor and imagination to invent problems. (3) Make a handout of two to five letters based on or chosen from the problem letters the students wrote. Have students write advice letters in reply. (4) Compile the students' problem letters and advice letters into a column for publication. Whenever necessary, combine similar letters or pad skimpy letters. Have students choose a name for their advice column and draw a picture of the adviser.

Potpourri   Have students write articles on one or more of these topics: recipes/descriptions of typical meals and dishes from students' countries; reviews of restaurants that serve the students' native foods; restaurant/food opinion poll in which students interview teachers and others about their favorite restaurants or recipes; and reviews or polls about current or all-time movie, book, or record favorites or worsts.

PUBLISHING AND READING THE NEWSPAPER

In-class activities   Give students some time to look over the whole issue silently. Then ask questions based on information scattered throughout the issue. Have students respond to each question by giving only the number of the page and headline of the article where they would *look for* the the answer. Hand out a list of the *same* questions with a space for each answer and its page number. See who can find all of the information first. Next, have students write two to four questions of their own, each on a slip of paper. Ask students to put their names on the strips too. Make two teams, and draw the students' questions from a bag. Read the questions, and give points for correct answers. Read any malformed questions correctly without mentioning that there was any error. Finally, do the cloze exercise if you have used such a format in typing up one of the articles. Work the crossword puzzle, and enjoy your collective accomplishment.

Publication reception   When the newspaper is finished, organize a reception for at least two or three guests. Send invitations, written of course, to another class, the director, the school secretary, and/or other sympathetic people. Plan and rehearse a short program with a student acting as the master of ceremonies, and other students presenting/ reading each newspaper selection. If possible, snap a few photos and close with simple refreshments.

⟫→

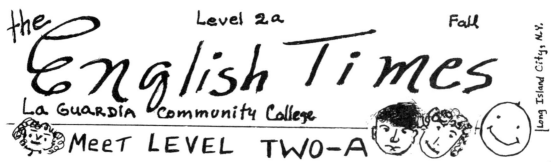

the English Times

Level 2a   Fall

Long Island City, N.Y.

La GUARDIA Community College

MeeT LEVEL TWO-A

Sixteen students, 10 females and 6 males, ___ in the level-2A class at LaGuardia Community College. They _____ from 8 countries in ____, Africa, America, and Europe. They _____ the following native languages: Arabic, Chinese, Greek, Korean, Spanish, and Tigre. In _____ countries they had various occupations. Twelve of them ____ students. Other occupations included beautician, electrical technician, and driver.

The students _____ in age from 20 to 41 years. The _____ age is 28.7 years. One student has been in the U.S. ____ 9½ years.

Others have been here for only two months. The _____ length of time in the U.S. is 3.75 years.

Six of the students ____ married. Only three students _____ alone. The others live with their spouses and/or relatives.

_____ teachers work with the level-2A class: Drena Contreras, Beverly Ingram, and Susan _____. According to these teachers, the class, on the whole, _____ hard and cooperates well. The teachers _____, " It is really a pleasure to work with such a lovely group of people."

LEVEL TWO VISITS ZOO

Eleven level-two _____ from La Guardia College _____ to the Bronx Zoo on May 22. About 9:45 a.m. Tracey and the students _____ La Guardia and _____ at the zoo about 11 a.m. It _____ a long time to arrive at the zoo _____ the group started late from school, and the zoo was far. Beverly and _____ son, Kevin, _____ waiting at the zoo entrance. Kids were everywhere because _____ is free on Tuesdays. Nicolas and Nader arrived later, just before lunch, because they had trouble with the _____. They found the group because they saw Tracey on a bench near the cable ____.

In the morning the students walked around the zoo in small groups, took photos, and looked _____ the animals. The group ____

Cont. pg. 2*

An Important Lesson

Two weeks ago I went to 34th St. to a big store to buy a wool skirt for winter. I had three or four hundred dollars in my handbag. While I was waiting at the cashier to buy the skirt, I didn't find the money. My handbag was open. The money was gone. I felt afraid. I didn't buy the skirt.

Before this experience took place in my life, I wasn't nervous. I'm very careful now. I carry my handbag in front of me, not behind. This day was very instructive for me.   -Aouatif Zerrad-Hyalouki-

TODAY'S WEATHER

Clear, sunny skies, day time high: 75°F, low tonight: 60°F

P.S To enjoy today's weather go to El Valle, Colombia, in June.

Reporter: Edilma Torres

*Page 2 is not shown here.

WHAT'S MY CITY ?

3

Reporters: Jose Cardenas, Jorge Castro, Nuo Cen, Michael Damianou, Chong Hak Kong, Ethel Osorio, Juan Carlos Prieto

Test your knowledge of travel and geography. Match the city and its description. Put the numbers in the blanks below. Good luck! (Check your answers on page **1** .)

1. Canton (China)
2. Choulou (Cyprus)
3. Estepona (Spain)
4. Inchon (Korea)
5. Medellin (Colombia)
6. Palmira (Colombia)
7. Santa Marta (Colombia)

____ A. It takes 50 minutes by train to go from my city to the capital. The principal product is salt.

____ B. My city is small, but very beautiful because of the beach. It is one of my country's most important seaports on the Atlantic Ocean.

____ C. Five hundred people live in my town. The land there is hilly and good for farming.

____ D. My city is situated between mountains in a valley crossed by a medium river. Its botanical gardens, especially the orchids, are famous.

____ E. My city has a long history. It has many famous universities and buildings. It also has many, many food factories. In the spring the ground is full of flowers. My city's other name is "flower city."

____ F. My city is in a valley in the south of my country. The principal industry is sugar cane and other agriculture.

____ G. My city is called "the sun of the coast." The principal industry is tourism. All of the city is interesting because of the Arabic architecture.

The Tank was Empty

Six years ago I lived in Athens. Every fifteen days I went to my village with my friend who had a new Italian car. One Friday the engine didn't work. My friend got out of his car and looked at it. He didn't see anything. For one hour he and I looked everywhere. We checked everything. Finally, after one hour we looked in the gas tank. It didn't have any gasoline! My friend and I felt terrible because the day before he had filled the tank, and today, it didn't have any gasoline. Anyway, together we put gasoline in the tank and went to my village. In the end my friend was lucky because the thief took only the gasoline. He still has his car.

-John Lapatsanis-

the Robbery

Last month I went shopping and saw a robbery. I saw it because I was inside shopping. A bad man took a lot of jewelry and stole other things. It was important to me because I saw a bad thing done. A policeman saw the bad man and stopped him. I was very sad because it was real, and it wasn't good. -Ana Clara Restrepo-

An Afraid Night

When I had just come to New York, I was not afraid when I walked home at night. One thing happened to my good friend to change me. One night, my good friend was going home after work. She was walking on the sidewalk. There were no people or cars in the street. Suddenly, a tall man jumped out of a doorway to come near her. He pulled out a sharp knife. He took her new handbag and expensive watch. He left. My friend did not say anything because she was very afraid. She lost a watch that cost $200 and $50 in money. After that, my friend didn't walk on the sidewalk at night. She bought a car to drive home. When my friend told me this dangerous thing, I was very afraid. Now I don't walk home at night. I'm very careful at night. -Xiao-He Zhao-

ENGLISH TIMES

Fall
Level 2a

Appendix 2: Editing Symbols

Symbols for mistakes in grammar and mechanics

Symbol	Explanation	Sentence marked with symbols	Corrected sentence
1. ⟨sp⟩	spelling error	Bev and Carol are teechers.	Bev and Carol are teachers.
2. ‿	Connect and make one word.	They like to work to gether.	They like to work together.
3. ⌃	Add something.	They ⌃ born in Texas.	They were born in Texas.
4. /	Omit this.	They are a good friends.	They are good friends.
5. ww	wrong word	Carol lives at Austin, Texas.	Carol lives in Austin, Texas.
6. wf	right word, wrong form	Both of them enjoy teach.	Both of them enjoy teaching.
7. #	number error, singular↔plural	They met fifteen year ago.	They met fifteen years ago.
8. poss	Use possessive form.	Bev home is now in New York City.	Bev's home is now in New York City.
9. vt	verb tense error	Carol work in Malaysia in 1986.	Carol worked in Malaysia in 1986.
10. sv agr	subject-verb agreement error	Bev have two sons.	Bev has two sons.
11. pro agr	pronoun agreement error	Carol always enjoys himself at parties.	Carol always enjoys herself at parties.
12. rep	repetition	Every day Carol has coffee daily.	Every day Carol has coffee.
13. ⌐‾	word order error	They taught in Algeria English.	They taught English in Algeria.
14. c, ¢	capitalization error	both of them like Languages.	Both of them like languages.
15. P, ⫽	punctuation error	They both, speak French	They both speak French.

16. ( )^R	run-on sentence	(Bev taught in Mexico, it was great.)^R	Bev taught in Mexico. It was great.
17. ( )^F	fragment error	(After they taught French.)^F	After college they taught French.
18. ¶, ¶	paragraph error		

Symbols for types of words

19. S	subject	⑤ ∧Worked in Tunisia.	Carol worked in Tunisia.
20. V	verb	ⓥ Carol ∧also a lawyer.	Carol is also a lawyer.
21. *aux*	auxiliary verb	(aux) Where ∧Bev learn Spanish?	Where did Bev learn Spanish?
22. *pron*	pronoun	(pron) Bev loves ∧husband very much.	Bev loves her husband very much.
23. *prep*	preposition	(prep) In 1983 they went ∧Toronto.	In 1983 they went to Toronto.
24. *art*	article	(art) Bev wants to take ∧trip to Brazil.	Bev wants to take a trip to Brazil.
25. *adj*	adjective	Carol and Bev wrote a (wf, use adj) wonderfully book.	Carol and Bev wrote a wonderful book.
26. *adv*	adverb	Carol and Bev make friends (wf, use adv) quick.	Carol and Bev make friends quickly.
27. *conj*	conjunction	Both of them like Chinese, (conj) ∧ Japanese, Thai food.	Both of them like Chinese, Japanese, and Thai food.

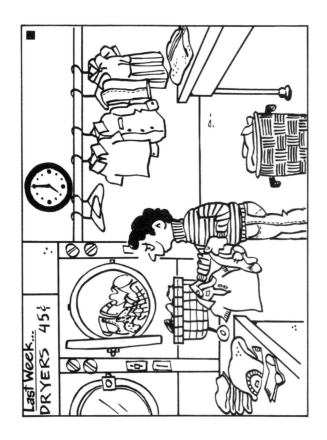

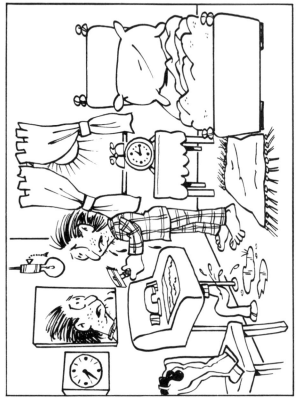